Th
Scrapper's
Way

Praise for *The Scrapper's Way*

The Scrapper's Way is a testament to a boy from a quaint Odisha village who soared to global heights yet remained deeply rooted in his origins. Dive into these pages and discover a leader whose heart beats to native rhythms yet whose spirit commands the respect of the corporate world.

—**Gopichand Katragadda**
Founder and CEO, Myelin Foundry; former MD, GE JFWTC

The Scrapper's Way weaves a gripping narrative of authenticity, intellect and empathy. Damodar gives the reader a choice to enjoy it as an enriching story, a primer for parenting, or even a reflective journal of self-awareness.

—**Emmanuel David**
Former director, Tata Management Training Centre

Browsing through the manuscript and learning about how Damodar has navigated the fork points in his life all along, *The Scrapper's Way* sometimes left me in splits, sometimes in tears, and sometime in complete awe.

—**P.R. Krishnan**
Former executive vice president, TCS

The Scrapper's Way is a journey of dreams and determination. This is the inspiring tale of one individual's unwavering pursuit of success against all odds. A remarkable journey of resilience and triumph!

—**Aarif Aziz**
Head of human resources, DIAGEO–Europe Region

Looking for a cookbook to success and happiness in life? Turn the pages of *The Scrapper's Way* … A must-read for aspiring students, working professionals and parents alike!

—**Ravi Viswanathan**
Joint MD, TVS Supply Chain Solutions Limited

Do not blame your circumstances. Give it a try. Advancing in your career and deriving sustained pleasure from life are in your hands! Damodar bespeaks this philosophy through authentic storytelling in this book.

—**Ritu Anand**
Former chief leadership and diversity officer, TCS

The

MAKING IT BIG IN AN
UNEQUAL WORLD

Scrapper's

Way

DAMODAR PADHI

HARPER
BUSINESS

An Imprint of HarperCollins *Publishers*

First published in India by Harper Business 2024
An imprint of HarperCollins *Publishers*
4th Floor, Tower A, Building No. 10, DLF Cyber City,
DLF Phase II, Gurugram, Haryana – 122002
www.harpercollins.co.in

2 4 6 8 10 9 7 5 3 1

P-ISBN: 978-93-5699-993-0
E-ISBN: 978-93-5699-987-9

Typeset in 11.5/15.7 Minion Pro at
Manipal Technologies Limited, Manipal

Printed and bound at
Thomson Press (India) Ltd.

MIX
Paper from
responsible sources
FSC® C010615

This book is produced from independently certified FSC® paper
to ensure responsible forest management.

*To my beloved parents, Rajuna and Kaka, for their love,
and to my siblings and Nuabou for their sacrifices*

The detailed references pertaining to this book are available on the HarperCollins *Publishers* India website. Scan this QR code to access the same.

CONTENTS

Foreword by S. Ramadorai   ix

Prologue   xiii

1. Tracing the Roots   1

2. Self-Awakening   28

3. Call of the Gurukul   36

4. Experiencing the Magnificent Ravenshaw College   63

5. Metamorphosis at REC Rourkela   90

6. IIT Kharagpur: Where the Dream Took Wing   117

7. In Pursuit of the Dream Job   122

8. The Leadership Journey   139

9. Fatherhood   158

10. Rediscovering the Self   177

11. Life in an Empty Nest   195

12. Through the Rearview Mirror   210

Acknowledgements   219

References   221

Index   223

FOREWORD

U PON BEING APPROACHED BY DAMODAR Padhi to write the foreword to this book, I travelled down memory lane to an evening function organized at the rooftop of the Tata Consultancy Services (TCS) office in Habibullah Road, Chennai (then called Madras). It was 1996, and he had just returned from the United States after solving a complex technical assignment with one of our long-cherished yet demanding customers, General Electric (GE).

Damodar continued to do well and earned my approval to lead a joint venture start-up between TCS and GE, named the Engineering Analysis Center of Excellence (EACoE). As the CEO and MD of TCS, and as a member of the EACoE board, I had the opportunity to observe Damodar closely. It was during these occasions that I recognized his potential as a professional, and encouraged him to keep learning and contributing to a larger purpose. He opted to move to GE as per the contract, but promised to return to TCS a few years later, if we found his learnings relevant and useful. He did, and TCS welcomed him back, entrusting him with the role of the global head of its learning and development function.

As I reminisce about his leadership, business and technical acumen, I am reminded of his humble background, which makes his achievements even more remarkable—a testament to the true scrapper's way.

However, writing a foreword to his book requires knowing Damodar on a more personal level. I, therefore, asked for a copy of the manuscript. As I browsed through the first few pages, the moving stories in the book began to grip me. Rural upbringing in a remote village in the coastal state of Odisha, a self-inspired attitude right from childhood, embracing life as it comes with a smile on the face, crafting a bright future for himself while lifting up thousands of budding professionals along his career journey—Damodar's book is all about aspirational India.

In the course of my professional life, and during my tenure as the chairman of the National Skill Development Corporation, I have come across many youth from rural or semi-urban backgrounds who were born to underprivileged families. It is not that the socioeconomic circumstances weathered by Damodar are totally unique to him; many children, especially in rural India, face similar adversity. Many lose their way during childhood, while others, who make it through school, struggle to land a job. Many of those who find a job struggle to find a purpose, and therefore, stagnate in their careers. There are many successful professionals who end up being unfulfilling parents.

Through intriguing storytelling, Damodar traces the continuity, and lets readers partake in the complex journey of his life. His stories will advise young and old alike to never give up in life, assuring them that if someone was not born with a silver spoon, it is not the end of the world.

The stories will further inform working professionals not to be obsessed with so-called dream jobs, but to live their dreams through every job that comes their way. There are many inspirational stories on parenting too.

I noticed one unique aspect that made this book a page-turner for me—there is absolutely no preaching. While the stories are personal, at a human level, everyone can relate and empathize with them, even if they are from totally different circumstances. Damodar's passion to influence and improve the ecosystem around him is evident in his endeavours.

I wish the book a wide readership.

S. Ramadorai

PROLOGUE

IT WAS 3 OCTOBER 2017. The *Chief Learning Officer (CLO)* international magazine had conferred on me the CLO of the Year award at a glittering gala held at the Hyatt Regency Huntington Beach Resort and Spa in California, USA. I was invited to receive the award in person.

My son, Suman Kalyan Padhi, nicknamed Ashish, was in his senior year at the University of California, Los Angeles (UCLA) then. Being within an hour's drive, I had asked him to come down for a sleepover so that we could catch up. At night, I enquired about his studies and the companies he was applying to for his first job on campus. He enquired about the award I had received earlier that evening. I had serious jet lag and blabbered something, before drifting off to deep sleep.

The CLO magazine was quick enough to announce the award on its LinkedIn handle the same night as the award function. I woke up to over a hundred notifications; many of my connections, including some senior colleagues and role models from current and previous organizations, had sent congratulatory messages. I had finished taking my bath by the time Ashish woke up. Being one of my connections on LinkedIn, he had also received the notification about me receiving the CLO award. Intrigued, he explored the URL to learn more about the award. I told him that we could talk about it later, in the car, and that he should first get ready so that I could drop him off at his college, en route the airport, where I would catch a flight to Washington D.C.

We booked an Uber. In the car, Ashish browsed through a few pictures that had been clicked on my iPhone during the event the previous night. He then urged me to write a book on my life story. 'Why?' I asked. 'It will surely inspire my generation,' he said.

Writing a book was the last thing on my mind, though many of my colleagues at Tata Consultancy Services (TCS) had been insisting on it. 'Daddy, I am forwarding you a write-up right away. I wrote it four years ago as the personal statement for my college applications. I had not told you earlier, nor do I need to flatter you now. But everything I wrote in the personal statement is my true impression of you. I want you to read it, please. After that, if you are still not convinced about writing a book, let us talk about it again,' Ashish said.

It was quite unusual for him. I had never seen him as persuasive, except when he wanted some money out of me, or when he anticipated me pushing back on some of his extravagant desires. Curiously, I downloaded the write-up and saved it for in-flight reading.

Here's what he had written:

My father grew up with two pairs of clothes at any given point of his childhood, poor even for a kid brought up in rural India in the 1960s. His daily rituals began with taking care of his sanitary activities in the nearby woods followed by a swim in

the river that he had to cross on his way to school. Following
this three-mile hike to his school, he would reap the benefits
that the harsh, unforgiving ways of the Indian education system
offered. His desire for knowledge and success did not waver as
he faced this childhood without once considering the easy way
out. He defied the odds, over and over again, eventually making
it to the Indian Institute of Technology through a gruelling
admissions process that makes the odds I face today, applying
to schools as selective as yours, seem exceedingly generous.
But he is still the same hard-working, brilliant, humble man,
who was able to overcome his circumstances. And it is this that
I must live up to, if not surpass. Every trip to my paternal or
maternal village reminds me of my father's legacy: people look
at me and murmur (a rough translation), 'Is that Dama's (my
father's nickname) son?' 'He looks so much like him.' 'He has
his dad's charisma.' 'He will do great things.' To me, it all sounds
like the stuff of fairytales when I look at it on paper, but that
is the situation I find myself in. I have a father who embodies
the rags-to-riches archetype, and it is he whose reputation I
must live up to.

This pressure to live up to him is an integral part of my
identity. It is the exposure that has resulted in all this pressure,
which has given me an idea of how fortunate I am and how
few excuses I have to not succeed. I can never hope to compare
myself to him, for it would be unfair to him for me to even
pretend like I overcame the same hostile childhood he did. His
circumstances were not exactly ideal for a student, considering
the lack of electricity, running water and resources, both
monetary and academic. My excess on all of those accounts
during my childhood, complemented with my frequent trips
to my parents' villages, have put me in a unique situation where

I have an abundance of the necessary resources, but have learnt not to abuse them. My grandparents have witnessed their son overcome overwhelming odds to become the great, philanthropic man who has delivered numerous favours to people in and around his village; a man who resembled me quite a lot as he grew up. They now expect nothing short of proportional greatness from me. And considering my fortunate childhood, the pressure is on.

I have come to realize that there is no reason for me to not surpass his legacy. I have been blessed with so much that he had not, and all because of him. I have thus come to terms with the fact that the most pressure I face is the pressure I have come to put upon myself due to my complete understanding of my blessed nature. It is this that helps me view the world so rationally. Once you come to terms with your blessed circumstances, you stop making excuses. You start being accountable for your actions and failures, and this helps you grow as a person exponentially, and I can think of no better example than myself. I am my biggest critic, and it is this that has helped me grow in all my activities, from Model UN to coaching my MathCounts team.

In a sense, my father faced a similar, if not greater, degree of pressure; his motivation was rooted as much from a desire to help himself and his family. He knew the only way out of poverty was to succeed academically, and the only path to success was the sheer diligence and perseverance that he portrayed. He wanted to improve not only his life, but also the life of his extended family and the people who helped him along his life journey. I have learnt from this.

The pressure I feel is self-imposed, as I take the expectations others set for me as a source of motivation. Wanting, and being expected, to live up to my father's reputation is not a negative pressure that has ever brought me close to feeling nervous, but it is a source of inspiration. Wealth is no longer my goal. If wealth is a consequence of my actions, or even a stepping-stone to make my ambitions more attainable, so be it. He portrays his belief convincingly, that those who chase money do not make that much, but those who intend to excel at what they do can make a lot. To excel I shall try, but to help others with myself.

It was a challenge to hide my face from my co-passenger; I could not control my tears. All along, Ashish liked to play with me—cricket, badminton, table tennis, and sometimes even swimming in the pool—but whenever I pushed him to study, he would evade it, making up some excuses. Once, he even pushed back rebelliously, saying 'did you ever have fun while you were in school, Daddy?' Growing up, the same boy, in his personal statement, projects me as his role model!

There are nuances in his goal statement that can be debated. However, the larger truth, as I saw, was that he had derived inspiration from my life story. I had never narrated my story to him—whatever he knew about me was from listening to my parents, and by observing me and my wife over a period of time.

The attributes that Ashish touched upon in his write-up are typically the attributes of a scrapper, one who is resilient and persistent, who fights and strives to succeed against all odds, without making any excuses. This is the scrapper's way.

I never liked the thought of writing an autobiography, as most autobiographies about people from humble beginnings, rising through the ranks, usually carry one central message: the extraordinary qualities of the protagonist, being born to a poor family, sometimes even in a hostile environment, yet rising to greatness through sheer personal effort. It's the story of the 'self-made man'. Such stories are fascinating, but I feel they transcend to a level beyond the capabilities of common man; so much so, that people might not even try to emulate.

I feel differently about life. In my view, anyone can make it reasonably big. If someone was not born with a silver spoon, it is not the end of the world. One does not need to be a superman either. No one is. That is why I chose to write about my own life story. I believe it will inspire the readers, as I have a different story to tell.

1

TRACING THE ROOTS

THE MEMORY OF MY VILLAGE makes me admire the unknown architect who conceived its blueprint. The serenity surrounding a vast pond, fondly called the Hensanaga, instils calmness in the turbulent minds of the digital age. The village school situated in its southwest corner; tall tamarind trees growing on its banks of the pond in the west and northwest corner; a lone gigantic banyan tree standing to the north, and the splendour of their reflection in the water takes one's breath away.

The village is oriented east-west in a perfect straight line. Towards the east, it extends to an ancient pipal tree that gives shelter to Goddess Jagulei; on the west, it is crowned by the temple of Grameshwara Mahadeva. Goddess Jagulei does not yet have a roof over her head—she has been content while wedged against the main trunk of the pipal, which itself has seen several incarnations, shapes and sizes, having been struck by cyclones from time to time. The Mahadeva temple premises, on the other hand, has been enhanced in stages over the last few decades to include an entrance (the Mukhashala), a Hanuman temple, a kitchen, a tube well, a room for housing the Trinatha idol, and other puja utensils.

This is Mahanga, my adorable little village, which falls under Niali block in the district of Cuttack, in the eastern Indian state of Odisha.

Whenever I visit my village, I try to stick to this one ritual as far as possible: go to the rooftop in the morning and witness the gorgeous panorama of the sun rising on Goddess Jagulei, then gaze at the setting sun over the Grameshwara Mahadeva temple.

Going to the rooftop was never an option in my childhood; neither my house nor any other in the village had a concrete roof. There were two facing rows of adobe houses with thatched roofs, separated by a fifteen-feet pathway in the middle, called the village danda. It is now cemented, but back then, it was a typical walkway made of mud, with its own seasonal look and feel. In the winter and summer, it would be more even, with dust and sand loosened up by the hooves of cows, calves, and bullocks. In the rainy season, rainwater sliding down the inclined thatched roofs on both sides gradually eroded them, creating a stream in the middle.

Speaking of the rainy season, the first thing every kid in our village would learn was to make a paper boat. The scene that's etched in my memory is that of my friends and me, with paper boats that we had made poised in our hands, impatiently waiting for the rain to stop so that we could carefully lower them into the rushing stream. We clapped in glee as we watched them bobbing downstream, crossing one house after another.

Let alone the seasons, the danda looked different at various times of the day. Almost every household had domestic animals, mostly cows and bullocks. Some had sheep and goats. Early in the morning, they were released from their sheds, escorted to the danda, and tied down with a rope to a series of pegs on either side.

After spending the night in dark sheds, they would enjoy the early morning sunshine while their sheds were cleaned.

The danda was a 'happening' place every morning. Sitting on the veranda, I used to watch various activities: cows being milked as they enjoyed their morning feed (usually a small pile of hay); bullocks being fed paddy husk before they got paired and their shoulders loaded with ploughs; women and girls taking early morning dips in the Hensanaga pond and walking along the danda after offering prayers to Grameshwara Mahadeva; boys of different age groups in huddles, planning simple games for the morning— usually a game of marbles—and being shouted at by parents for not studying or engaging in household activities.

By the time the children went to school, all the animals were untied and escorted to the common non-agricultural lands in the village. Our village shamshana (cremation ground), the school ground, the embankments of the canal and the Hensanaga pond, and the curvy contour of Marichia Nali—a water body that flowed through the agricultural lands of our village—together provided abundant common wasteland. Right from the onset of monsoon until the end of winter, weeds and grasses of different kinds grew in ample quantities and served as fodder. Children from poor families who could not afford to continue their studies, or those who dropped out because of consistent poor grades, were the ones who became cowherds, roaming the fields through the day.

The danda suddenly turned quiet after the children left for the fields or school. After sunset, the danda burst into life again, as groups of satiated cattle started lumbering back home, along with their cheerful cowherds, raising dust along the danda till it rose to the sky. This is precisely why twilight after sunset in most Indian rural areas is referred to as the godhuli ('go' meaning cow and 'dhuli' meaning dust) hour.

As an East Indian state, the sun sets quite early in Odisha, especially in winter. Electricity was unheard of back then. The village, therefore, used to fall into pin-drop silence just a couple of hours after dusk. Summer days were very hot and humid; most people, especially the young children, took naps in the afternoon. The evenings were relatively cooler; nightlife, therefore, used to extend a bit longer. The evening aarti in the temple was distinct and meticulously performed in all seasons. The evening Trinatha mela was a frequent social event, providing a source of engagement and entertainment for many. The sky reverberated whenever expert hands played cymbals and mridangams in synchronization, especially on the days of Dola Purnima and Kartika Purnima. The festivity around Durga puja, Ganesha puja and Saraswati puja was evident. During festivals like Raja Parba, Kumar Purnima, Khudurukuni puja, Dol Purnima and Boat Purnima, which are unique to Odisha, the village turned vivacious.

In this beautiful village, there lived a Brahmin community, known as the Padhis, who served as the priests to Goddess Jagulei and Grameshwara Mahadeva. The community, at some point in history, must have begun as a single family bearing the entire responsibility—and the benefit—of being priests to the village deities. But by the time I was born into this family, my father, Balakrishna Padhi (whom we called Nana), happened to be one of five brothers born to my grandfather, who himself was among three brothers born to my great-grandfather. The inheritance of the temple property and the privileges, therefore, were divided multiple times, making my father's share look rather small.

Nana was the youngest among his siblings. His youngest paternal uncle died of cancer at an early age, so the latter adopted Nana, his nephew, to take care of his wife (Maa) and their son (Kaka), who was an infant then. Nana had just got married. My mother (Bou) was young, inexperienced and bewildered, and therefore, did not participate in the discussion or exercise any choice; she just nodded and followed in Nana's footsteps when all these transitions were taking place.

By the time I was born, the family wasn't stricken by 'poverty' as such, as I do not have many recollections of long starving. But we were in the grips of acute 'scarcity'. My memory goes back to four years of age, and at the time, we were a family of seven—Nana, Bou, Maa, Kaka, my older brother (Bhaina), older sister (Sanjunani) and I. We had just two rooms and one kitchen for the seven of us, and one shed for the household animals—two bullocks, a cow and a few calves. All these units had mud flooring and thatched roofs standing on four walls made of clay. I never saw a tractor in my entire childhood; bullocks were used to power wooden ploughs to cultivate agricultural land. In fact, the number, size and health of the bullocks owned by a family were indeed the indicators of its overall wellness.

During the day, there was no concept of privacy, and everyone used every room. At night, Kaka and Maa slept in one room, Nana and Bhaina in the other room, and Bou and Sanjunani in the kitchen. Don't ask about me. I had free access to all the rooms, but with one condition: once I made up my mind and the doors were closed, I was stuck, and it was a difficult task to change rooms. It wasn't though there was some sort of ordinance in our home, just that everyone except me was so tired doing chores all day that they fell into deep sleep soon after finishing supper.

I have overheard Bou narrating a story from my childhood to her grandchildren a few times:

Once I had accompanied Bou to visit Rohit Mamu, one of my maternal uncles, in Cuttack. That was the first time I travelled in a bus. The story is not about the bus journey; rather, it is about my troubles with my morning ritual. Rohit Mamu made me squat on the toilet seat (an 'eastern' or 'Indian-style' toilet, as it is called), closed the door and left. I had never been in a situation where I could do my business on such a clean surface in a confined room. Feeling awkward, I left the bathroom right after Mamu and reached out to Bou, asking how I could dirty such a clean room? She made me squat again, saying, 'this is where you have to'. But this time, she left the door open and waited there until I struggled through my ritual in vain. The task was abandoned when I declared I couldn't. The whole day passed, but I still couldn't, until the right conditions came about the next day. Bou and Mamu took me to a big playground a few blocks away from his residence. Fenced by trees of various kinds, such a huge open space overlooking the river Mahanadi offered the right vibe for doing my thing. The whole experience was easy and soothing, with perfect ventilation and natural lighting. What else? I cleaned myself in the river and skipped back home with Bou and Mamu. The next morning, I urged Bou to escort me to the same place again!

This other anecdote is my personal favourite though: the story commenced early in the morning following my fourth birthday. I woke to everyone at home crying. Unconcerned, I stared at everyone, and then walked straight to our courtyard to take a good look at the pants I was wearing—a birthday gift from my maternal uncle. I had not noticed the colour of the pants, as it had been quite dark by the time they had arrived the previous night. I then went inside the kitchen and grabbed a small stack of pooris that was preserved by Bou, for me, from the previous night. Poori, as a special dish, was not a feature of my birthday feast, but that year, my birthday coincided with Dussehra, the only day of the year when Bou made poori at home for supper. By the time the pooris were ready, I had slept off. But Bou, true to her word, had secretly hidden a few pooris for me exactly where I had asked her to. I put the pooris in my pocket and showed off my new pants to everyone I came across while munching one poori after another. Everyone was still crying. Confused, I asked why they all were crying. Sanjunani said an elderly person in our extended family had died. I had a 'so what?' look on my face, but Sanjunani and Bhaina asked me to cry too. 'Why should I cry?' I wondered, looking at them with my hands in my pocket. 'Let me enjoy my poori,' I added with a smile. Both cracked up.

However, soon after, they dragged me to a room where many other people had already assembled to pay homage to the departed soul; they forced me to join them in crying.

Nana was a smallpox survivor; he had scars from the lesions all over his body. That was not the only reason he appeared scary to me; I rarely saw him laugh. Moreover, I had noticed him thrashing Bhaina a few times. I therefore never preferred to sleep in the room where he and Bhaina used to sleep. Sometimes, I slept alongside Bou and Sanjunani, but most nights, I slept with Maa and Kaka. Kaka used to tell nice bedtime stories. But there was another reason why I opted to sleep with them; I remember, as a child, I would wet the bed, and it took a rather long time to grow out of the habit. And Kaka, who had a sort of inexplicable love for me, let me sleep there regularly despite my bedwetting. He would never punish me. Once he felt the bed was wet, he would wake up grudgingly, increase the flame of the kerosene lantern, wake me up, rebuke me a little, change my wet pants, wrap me with whatever he could lay his hands on, reduce the lantern flame, cuddle me, and go back to sleep.

When my younger sister Rita was born, I was five years old. Kaka was in high school, Bhaina in primary school and Sanjunani in elementary school. Sanjunani dropped out by the time I started going to the school. It wasn't that she was bad at studies, but our village school only taught up to the third standard, and to go to the nearest primary school in another village, she would have had to join Bhaina in a three-kilometre walk each way. That was an impossible task for her, as by the time she was nine, she had already taken over half the household responsibilities from Bou.

You must be wondering what Bou was up to. In my memory, she was the most hardworking woman in our entire village. She joined Nana in most of the chores, like working in the betel leaf farm, which would normally be done by male members in other families, and also doing her own chores like preparing cow dung cakes and collecting cooking fuel from the nearby woods. Ladies from Brahmin families were prohibited from doing certain activities, or else she would have probably joined Nana at the paddy fields as well.

As far as I can remember, a typical day for all our family members was quite different from the rest of the families in our village. Unlike boys of similar age groups who were seen either with books or on playgrounds, Kaka and Bhaina helped Nana in the paddy fields, or with betel leaf farming, when they were not at school. They did so every day for a couple of hours each in the morning and evening. While they were at school, Bou would help Nana, leaving the responsibility of taking care of Rita in the hands of Sanjunani. I returned from our village school around noon. Sanjunani then handed over Rita to me and focused on finishing the remaining work in the kitchen. Her responsibilities also included fetching water and storing it for drinking and cooking. There were no tube wells or hand pumps in the entire village. The only source of potable water was a handful of open wells. Using a rope, Sanjunani would draw water from the well in a gara (a brass pot), walk a hundred feet, including climbing a few steps up and down each way between the well and our kitchen, and begin filling up every vessel she could lay her hands on. She was a girl on a mission! She would exhaust the entire collection of vessels and lay her hands on the last tiny pot into which she could empty the last few ounces of water. If she found an empty one, all was well; if not, she would force me to open my mouth, pour in whatever water remained, and if needed, shake out the last few drops into her own mouth before running to the well with the gara in hand to draw the last pot of water for the day.

We had some agricultural land. Bou, Kaka and Bhaina were helping hands to Nana in farming, thereby reducing dependency on paid labour. On top of it, considering my father also functioned as a priest, thus having a side income, we should have been leading a reasonably easy life. But the reality was different. Nana and his older siblings were entangled in family feuds leading to multiple court cases, which dragged on for more than seven years, and drained significant resources. Every year, Nana borrowed money to fund the court cases, hoping to end them soon. But he eventually ended up just paying back the interest on the loan of previous years in addition to borrowing some more money to support the court cases in the upcoming year.

There was yet another problem. Once in every four to five years, the entire Mahanadi Delta region was affected by severe floods, ensuring complete destruction of kharif crops. So just when it seemed that things were settling down a bit, a flood would appear from nowhere and drag the family back by a few years. I was too young to understand all these dynamics. The only option for a confused five-year-old was simple: hold on to the pallu of Bou's saree and follow her wherever she went.

Bou visited her father's home often during festivals, and occasionally some other times as well, to borrow funds. I invariably accompanied her on those visits. Bou's interest and knowledge in mythology was beyond my comprehension. She had never gone to school, but had taught herself to be fluent in reciting and explaining the epics, the Ramayana and the Mahabharata, to villagers. As soon as she reached, the news would spread, and in the evening, people would flock in large numbers to my grandfather's courtyard to listen to Bou. I would sit beside Bou and listen to the stories. At that tender age, the stories of the demon king Ravana flying in his Pushpak Vimana all the way from Lanka to Dandaka Forest to abduct Sita, Hanuman flying across the ocean and locating Sita in Ashoka Vatika and setting the entire island on fire, the golden deer Marich, Jatayu bird and Shabari were just fascinating. My favourite character in Ramayana, however, was that enthusiastic squirrel who would ardently jump into the ocean, swim back to the shore, and roll over the sand, run all the way on the Rama Setu, shaking its body to shed those few grains of sand. I was amused to hear Bou explaining that the imprints on the back of a squirrel are indeed the stroking of Rama's fingers, in appreciation for its love and dedication.

'Why did Ravana kidnap Sita? Why did only Ravana have a Pushpak Vimana and not Rama? If Rama was a God, why could he not anticipate Ravana's ploy to kidnap Sita?' I would ask Bou all these questions, but the more she explained, the more my curiosity grew.

I would ask Bou questions on all spheres of life. One day, we set out to pluck vegetables from the small garden in our backyard. Bou noticed when I was about to pluck a baby vegetable. 'It is not yet the right time to pluck that one,' she said with a hint of irritation on her face. I stopped and felt disappointed, but I became curious.

'What is the right time to pluck a vegetable, Bou?'

'When you feel that it has stopped growing,' she explained.

From that day on, my thinking changed. I no longer asked Bou about whether it was the right time to pluck a particular vegetable or not. I asked, rather, to help me judge whether the vegetable I was going to pluck had stopped growing.

For a child, learning is mostly the result of imitating parents, relatives and elder siblings: like we learn to walk, run and speak. Being inquisitive accelerates learning. Just as I learnt from Bou about plucking vegetables, I picked up several other habits from situational experiences that have been hard-coded into my DNA.

What follows below is one such incident, in as much detail as I can remember:

Regular meals at home in my childhood comprised rice and dal, plus some sautéed vegetables. The rice, being homegrown, did not have a quantity cap. Dal, on the other hand, was on weekly ration, and hence, was portion-controlled, diluted enough to seamlessly seep through the pile of rice. Bou would continue pouring the dal until it oozed out at the base of the pile, culminating with a gratifying smile or a gentle shout—'enough'! Vegetables were homegrown but seasonal, so when we had them we felt good, and when not, we learnt to manage.

While eating, I had this habit of dragging rice to the edge of the plate while scooping out a portion, causing some rice to spill onto the floor. Nana had noticed this a few times. One day, he made me sit opposite him and eat from his plate. That day I ate with utmost caution, without dropping a single grain of rice. He patted my back with a parting remark, 'Good job today, I am sure from tomorrow you will not waste any food'.

Old habits die hard. Soon after, on a fateful day, Nana again noticed me dropping food on the floor. Giving me a scary look, he just dragged my plate away and showed me the mound of rice shaped like a crescent along the floor. He raised his hand to slap me, and I froze. Bou's plea stalled the slap mid-way. 'It is not customary to punish while eating. Forgive him this last time. He won't waste food again,' she said. However, I wasn't spared so easily. Not only did Nana make me eat the dropped food, but he also ensured zero waste. It felt disgusting to pick up the last few grains of rice off the mud floor. As an adult now, I know that deep within, he would not have felt happy that day, but he did not want to miss the opportunity to pass on an important learning. Learning from extreme experiences sticks in the mind, whether they are palatable or not. And soon, the learning develops into a habit.

With time, I was becoming increasingly aware of the constraints through which my parents were navigating our joint family. One day, Sanjunani was finishing cooking. Lunch, as usual, was in its simplest form: rice, dal and mashed brinjal. I was helping Sanjunani as it would help me get a relatively better portion of mashed brinjal. While she was busy seasoning the dal, I was peeling the roasted brinjal. Yes, 'brinjal' singular, not plural—one reasonably large brinjal for the entire family of seven. Rita was still a toddler, so did not count. Upon splitting and peeling it, I jumped back in disgust, as there was an insect, more than an inch long, dead inside! 'What happened?' asked Sanjunani anxiously. 'A big insect inside,' I said. Sanjunani didn't say a word. I could read the dilemma on her face. Neither could she tell me to throw the brinjal away, nor could she tell me to ignore the insect and carry on. We didn't have anything else to go with the rice and dal. There were no more brinjals left to roast. That is when I decided to take over. 'Look, the insect is dead! The brinjal must have been thoroughly sterilized when it was being roasted. Hence, we do not have to throw it away.' I built a convincing argument, throwing the insect away, and asking Sanjunani to carry on with the seasoning. Later, when Sanjunani served lunch for all of us, no one noticed, but I did—she had tears rolling down her face. One could not tell whether they were tears of helplessness at the situation, or tears of appreciation for the sensitive and supportive brother I was, at barely eight years old.

My home was different from many others in my village—it was the epitome of love and compassion. This next incident from fifty years ago defines this.

Like every other day, Sanjunani served me food before I sprinted off to my village school. I typically craved for a relatively larger portion of mashed potato seasoned with green chili and mustard oil, which really helped push the barely lubricated dal-rice down the throat. On that day, the portion of mashed potato was barely noticeable. 'This is mashed potato?' I sneered, then hurled the bowl at Sanjunani. Oh my God! One invariably hits the target when it is least desirable; the bowl struck her forehead. I saw her collapse on the floor, covering her forehead with her palm. She was bleeding. I was so afraid of being beaten up by my father that I fled to school on an empty stomach. It was a miserable day in school too; on top of the hunger, I was agonized at having hurt my sister. On my way back from school, I was thinking that Nana would surely have come to know about the incident, and I would have to suffer heavy punishment. But Sanjunani had lied to my father, saying she had stumbled in our backyard and had hurt her forehead.

There was one chore that I had seen Bou and Sanjunani do for most of my childhood: separating husk from paddy using the dhenki, an old-style manual device found in rural Odisha, to separate rice grains. I'm not sure whether an operational dhenki can be found in a household anymore (there are none in my own village), but it could guarantee a big draw in museums for sure. Back then, however, it was an integral part of most households. Apart from making rice, dhenki was also used for crushing oil cakes (pidia) to powder, for use as manure in betel leaf farming.

Having a dhenki was not a status symbol; rather, it signified an indigenous and industrious family that could not afford making rice out of paddy or crushing oil cakes using power-operated mills. We had a dhenki of our own, at the far end of our house, next to the shed that used to house our cows and bullocks. There was a saying that a dhenki was the most useful asset in a household that could not be stolen. Why? Because of its sheer size and weight! A dhenki consisted of a massive wooden log that served as a lever, which was supported on a fulcrum at one end. The other end was mounted with a piece of weight on to a pod. It was left unlocked, usually housed on the rear veranda. It was customary not to have walls on at least two of the four sides of the space as operating a dhenki called for adequate natural lighting. But having a thatched roof to protect it from rain was essential.

As a child, it was fascinating to just stand and watch how a dhenki worked. Kicking down on one end of the massive wooden log resulted in the other end first rising and then thudding on to a pile of paddy. Repeated cycles of thudding created a rhythmic sound, which reverberates in my ears even today. A single cycle—the hood of the dhenki rising to a height of three to four feet and thudding on to the pile of paddy below—took just about a second. Within this single second, Sanjunani would swiftly scoop out a portion of the partially beaten paddy in one hand, while feeding a similar portion of fresh paddy using the other hand. If there was even the slightest lack of coordination or concentration, the heavy pod would thud onto Sanjunani's palm. I was, therefore, allowed to just stand and watch, but to never indulge in talking to or distracting Sanjunani. One day, out of curiosity, I joined Bou in the rhythmic kicking of the dhenki. It appeared fun at the beginning, but soon I realized what a difficult job it was. The entire night I was in pain, and urged Maa to massage my aching right leg.

Maa was known as quite a character in our entire village. Growing up, I learnt that kids get addicted to grandmas' stories. I, however, had never noticed any children around Maa, except of course my sister Rita and myself. She scolded anybody and everybody for no apparent reason. Knowing her nature, nobody took her scolding seriously. People in the village just laughed her off and walked by. Everyone at home used to eat Pakhala—an Odia speciality of cooked rice washed or lightly fermented in water— except her. She was the only one who needed morning tea. Just black tea, we couldn't afford milk on a regular basis. She boiled her own cup of tea, refusing to drink it if anyone else prepared it. Along with her tea, she would have puffed rice, made of two fistfuls of rice. Just two fistfuls. Not a single grain more, not a single grain less. She grumbled if the puffed rice was not fresh, and fried her own every day. That, as such, was not the problem. But she was extremely slow. The ritual of her preparing her own tea and puffed rice consumed more than an hour every day. Other than that, I had never seen her doing any useful work. No one really liked her except Kaka and me. How could Kaka not like his own mother, and how could I not like my Maa? After all, I got my share of puffed rice from her, enriched my vocabulary in scolding, and more importantly, she let me sleep with her and Kaka at night.

Kaka was four years older than Bhaina. He was an expert in climbing trees, swimming in the Hensanaga pond and catching fish using rods. I derived pleasure in following him around and trying to emulate him. He would climb up the tall tamarind tree and shake its branches. Standing under the tree, I clapped gleefully, watching tamarind rain onto the ground. Each time he caught a fish, I was ecstatic, and kept fiddling with them long after he had put them securely inside the basket. For some reason, I never found Bhaina as exciting.

Emulating Kaka gradually became my way of life during childhood. I also began climbing small trees, and learnt to swim in the Hensanaga pond. Kaka taught me how to fish with a rod. Interestingly, Bou was quite skilled in catching fish too! It was quite a scene watching Bou and Kaka catch fish together from the small pond adjacent to our betel leaf farm, especially when the water levels in the pond and the adjacent water bodies receded during summer.

Once, an impromptu yet magnanimous act of Kaka's turned into a life lesson for me. Nana being a workaholic, it always fell upon Kaka to escort me and my siblings to this once-in-a-year Dipoti Melana—a famous festival in our neck of the woods—held on the day of Dol Purnima (the same day as Holi in North India, the full moon night of the month of Phalgun) every year. The journey involved crossing a river that would dry up after winter. Crossing that half-kilometre stretch was a daunting task for children, particularly in the afternoon, as the sand was scorching hot. And no one in our family wore footwear at the time.

My little sister Rita, only three years old, was comfortably seated on Kaka's shoulder. Sanjunani and I followed. After a few steps, Kaka looked behind to see me struggling to walk. He then did something unusual. I saw him scoop out the top two or three inches of the sand using his foot, as he took his steps. Then, turning back, he asked me to step exactly on the footmarks left behind by him. As I literally followed his footsteps, I realized how relatively cool the space was, even though it was just three inches beneath the surface of the original sand bed. Sanjunani followed me, and in about five minutes, we reached the other side of the river.

Time passes, life lessons don't. And in this case, impressions, cast on sand, made their way deep into the heart. 'Empathy is putting one's foot in another person's shoes,' preach management gurus. I learnt it quite early in life, from Kaka.

Amidst watching the squabbling between Nana and his siblings, accompanying Bou to my maternal grandfather's house, imitating Kaka, lending a helping hand to Sanjunani in household chores, seeing Bhaina, Kaka and Bou join Nana farming, the three years of my village elementary schooling just flew. I still remember the first black and white picture book of the Odia alphabet. In English, such a book would typically begin with A for apple, B for boy and so on, with the second half of the book illustrating formations of simple words and sentences. In Odia, the structure of the book was similar. Apart from recognizing letters of the Odia alphabet and reciting poems, I learnt simple addition, subtraction, multiplication and division. Going by what our school teacher told Bou and Kaka, I was good with numbers. To my glee.

Other than that, I cannot recollect much about what I studied in elementary school. But one learning that gradually developed into a childhood hobby, and perhaps into a subconscious force within, inspiring and guiding me later like a compass throughout my professional career and in life, was flying kites!

Kite-flying used to be customary in Odisha during the Raja Festival. Nana might have been a workaholic, but was a very different person when it came to this activity; it used to be his childhood hobby too. Year after year, I watched him teach the science and art of making kites to Bhaina. Slender twigs, chiselled from bamboo sticks and smoothened with a knife were used to make the frame. The number of twigs would have to be kept to a minimum, and they would need to be thin to make the kites as light as possible. 'Lighter kites soar higher,' Nana always used to remind Bhaina. Eight twigs were required for making smaller kites, twelve for larger ones. The outer four twigs must form a perfect rectangle.

To make sure that it is a perfect rectangle, both the diagonals must measure the same. The ratio of longer side to shorter side should be approximately 1.5. To make sure that you don't mess up, enough care needed to be taken while sizing the twigs in the first place, as also while tying the joints, especially the four corners and the centre. And most importantly, the two largest twigs used as diagonals would have to protrude by the same length, to make sure that you would eventually end up building a perfect rectangle and not a parallelogram; a sort of quality assurance testing, if you think of it! And all this coaching was by the father who had no formal education, did not know what a right angle, a rectangle or a parallelogram was. He just passed on what he himself had learnt by trial-and-error.

Despite all the lessons, my brother was unable to make good kites; this is still a subject we poke fun at. Each time, he would mess up something, resulting in a scolding from Nana. To add fuel to the fire, I would stand there and laugh. When chased, I would just run away.

One fine day, not sure how old I was, probably around seven, I tried playing around with the materials abandoned by Bhaina. Mentally replaying Nana's instructions, I started building a small kite, rectangular in shape, with eight twigs. After a few iterations, the frame appeared perfect by Nana's guidelines. I wrapped it with a piece of newspaper using glue, tied the balancing knot with three triangular threads (one each from the top two corners and the third from the centre), and attached a tail weight made from a small branch of a plant. It was time to test it out! I gathered a few friends, and off we sent the kite, to conquer the sky. And to our delight, it did! It may as well have been my heart soaring higher and higher instead of the kite; the feeling remains unparalleled till date, and the learning remains deep.

Following the announcement of school results, the school teacher enclosed in an envelope the list of students who had passed the elementary school exam and asked one of my classmates and me to deliver the envelope to the headmaster of a lower primary school, where we were supposed to eventually seek admission. This school was situated in another village, Kantapada, around three kilometres away. My classmate and I reached the school by around noon, and found the headmaster to be extremely affectionate and strict at the same time. He noticed that both of us were shirtless. Giving a stern look, he cautioned: 'You will not come to school without wearing a shirt. Do you understand?' We nodded our heads. On our way back, we looked at each other and burst out laughing uncontrollably. We never wore shirts in elementary school; in fact, I did not even have one! The ultimate in sartorial style had been wearing a vest while accompanying my mother to my maternal uncle's house.

My four years in the Kantapada school bring forth many vivid memories. Marichia Nali, a natural stream that originated from the river Prachi, one of the tail-end distributaries of the Mahanadi, flowed on the northern side of the village. The irrigation canal ran parallel to the village danda on the southern side. The rivalry between Marichia Nali and the canal was fascinating. Like its mother river Prachi, during the monsoon, the Marichia Nali swelled angrily and surged through its banks, flooding the entire stretch of paddy crops, creating havoc on the northern side of the village. The canal, on the other hand, played a nurturing role, supplying water to the winter and spring crops, and thanks to its embankments, providing the sole path for pedestrians, cyclists and the occasional motorized vehicles of nearly half-a-dozen villages in the area. In addition, its embankment arrested the water within the flooded canal, and prevented it from spreading to the southern side of the village.

There were two vulnerable spots in the five-kilometre-long canal. In the battle between the Marichia Nali exhibiting its might and the canal trying to resist the raging waters, often the Nali won. Apart from the impact on paddy crops, the residents of those half-a-dozen villages had a miserable time commuting from one village to another. The lives of schoolgoing children were challenging and yet amusing. Boys, walking to the school as a separate group, would just look back to ensure that girls were far away, smile playfully at each other, undress and cross the stream caused by the breach in the canal. Upon reaching the other side, they would wipe off their bodies using their own palms, put on the clothes, and carry on. Girls, travelling as another group, would be typically helped in crossing the canal by a male parent or an elder brother.

The canal embankment provided the sole means of transportation not only to pedestrians, but also to cattle and bullock carts. Due to heavy traffic, grass could never grow on the top surface of the canal embankments. For the entire rainy season, the clay on the walking surface simply became soft and slippery. Walking two and a half kilometres without slipping and tumbling was a challenge by itself. Add to it the task of protecting the books securely contained in a jute bag (plastic bags did not exist then) with one hand, while the other held up an umbrella. I had to be extra careful. If I happened to slip and tumble, the only option was to rinse off the affected area of my clothes and carry on to school. The option to return home, change clothes, and set out again did not exist; there were no spare clothes at home.

An incident from my days in Kantapada school leaves me with a deep sense of regret as well as enlightenment. It was on the day of Ganesh puja, a special day on which children were normally spared from daily chores, including studies. We woke up early in the morning, congregated in front of our village temple and went to pluck flowers, especially water lilies from the ponds and bell flowers of various kinds from neighbouring yards. While most of my buddies wore new clothes, I wore washed clothes that once belonged to my older brother, which I did for most of my primary school days. If the clothes were in decent shape by the time they were passed on to me, I had a smile on my face. We would then go to school to worship Lord Ganesha, so that he would grant us better grades in exams.

This particular day ended differently.

I was bored with the rituals of the previous years. On top of it, most other kids wore new clothes, except a very few, like me. Since attendance wasn't taken in school on Ganesh puja, there was no need to rush. So, I decided to play with a few like-minded friends in the morning instead of engaging in the annual chore of plucking flowers. We got engrossed in a hide-and-seek game in a neighbouring house. After playing for some time, my eyes fell on a brand new, unopened Lux Supreme soap on the table. I slipped the soap into my pocket, announced that the game was over, and hurried towards the pond to indulge in a luxurious bath.

I am not sure whether shampoos were being used in India then; I had never even used a soap to wash my hair before that day. Bou usually caught hold of me and forced a hair wash using washing soda and hot water, not when it was just untidy, but when it was so sticky that even simple combing became a daunting task. So, finding an unopened Lux Supreme soap was quite alluring.

I finished a supreme bath, my head feeling lighter and body smelling good. I felt like I had been reborn, and the day was set for a nice Ganesh puja. I approached home, dancing and whistling all the way. Hurtling through the tiny foyer, I stopped dead seeing

Nana sitting in the courtyard, facing the sun with a bottle in hand, massaging himself with oil before he headed for a bath. His eyes kept me rooted to the spot.

'Where did you get the soap from?' Nana asked.

'Bought it,' I replied in panic.

'Who gave you money?' he asked, his probing eyes scanning me from head to toe.

There was no point in continuing down the wrong path. I knew I was finished.

'I stole it from Oshi Maushi's house,' I said, surrendering, with my eyes downcast. I could feel the earth disappearing from under my feet as I saw him get up and close in on me.

A massive slap landed on my back. Seeing stars, I ran full speed to the neighbour's house, dropped the used soap on the table from where I had stolen it, and still running, blurted out, 'Oshi Maushi, I had stolen your soap, forgive me for my mistake'. I rushed back home at full speed and completed my sentence, 'Nana, I will never repeat this mistake for the rest of my life.'

Nana was still standing there. In his eyes, I saw the pain of not being able to afford a bathing soap for us. But he did not want to send conflicting messages; obstinately, he turned his face away.

I accepted internally that he had done the right thing by disciplining me.

Whenever I recall that incident, I can still sense Nana's stinging slap on my back. That is how life lessons are; they stand the test of time. Once imprinted, they can never be erased.

As time passed, a few other events unfolded. When I was nine years old, my youngest brother Shyama was born. Sensing scarcity, Kaka began offering tuitions to village children to raise some money to fund his studies. This added activity reduced his involvement in paddy cultivation and betel farming, for which

Nana and Bou ended up shouldering more responsibility. There was a scarcity of resources, but there was an abundance of empathy among the family members. Kaka soon realized that it was getting too difficult for Nana to shoulder the responsibility of the entire house, so he took the decision to drop out of school and support Nana full time in paddy cultivation and betel leaf farming. Scarcity had claimed its first victim in our joint family. But Kaka continued to offer tuitions to village children. I sat through those sessions, exhibiting an early interest in studies. The addition of more family members, especially with most children being young and growing, resulted in a food shortage.

For most of my childhood, we didn't have a regular side dish as part of our meals. From the proceeds of betel-leaf selling, Nana used to buy some potatoes and onions, along with other essential items like cooking oil and the cheapest available dal, once a week. The cash-strapped family didn't have the luxury of buying vegetables from the market. So, whenever Kaka caught some fish, the meals at home felt like a feast.

When Kaka got busy helping Nana with farming, he had no time left to catch fish. Not only did the family miss the taste of occasional fish curry, but I also experienced a sort of emptiness in me. The thrill of accompanying Kaka on those fishing expeditions was missing. One day, I took out Kaka's fishing rod that was gathering dust in the little courtyard, and set out to fish. This turned out to be one of my productive childhood hobbies.

By the time Bhaina started high school, he almost became a full-time help to Nana and Kaka in paddy cultivation and betel leaf farming. That certainly had an impact on his studies. He was a bright student with just one significant weakness—English. This he could not overcome, and eventually failed to clear the high school board exam. That put an end to his studies. Nana kept persuading him to retake the exam, in vain; Bhaina committed entirely to farming. Within three years, scarcity had claimed its second victim from the family.

At some point during my early years in primary school, Kaka had discontinued offering tuitions in the mornings. With that, the ritual of me opening study books in the morning had also stopped. After Nana, Kaka and Bhaina left for farming, I went out with my fishing rods, roaming around the water bodies in our village. But it didn't matter whether I caught more fish or less, we always had a good meal—Bou used to add some chopped potato, green chilli and mustard sauce, mix all the ingredients in a gina (small brass bowl), and place it on the residual fire after the main cooking got done, to prepare a delicacy, 'gina tarkari'. Delicacy means different things to different people: to most, it means fine, sophisticated cooking; but to Bou, it meant creative cooking amid scarcity.

Apart from catching fish, there was one more reason for which I was Bou and Sanjunani's pet: when adding a side dish to dal and rice was a challenge, tamarind pickle was the saviour. I was good at climbing trees, so I could go up the tamarind trees, swing from the branches like a monkey, and pluck out large quantities in very little time. Bou would stand watching me from the ground under the tree, cautioning me against climbing on or oscillating from thin branches, sometimes with her heart in her mouth. It was the same during the mango season, or while plucking flat beans from creepers that climbed onto roofs. I didn't even spare drumstick trees, knowing very well that their branches are indeed too brittle. These missions were aided by the fact that I was very thin; one could clearly count my ribs.

I was reasonably good at studies. That, however, did not get me respite from chores. Nana, Kaka and Bhaina did the difficult tasks; cleaning the weeds in the betel-leaf farm was considered a boring task for adults, but well-suited for my age and physical ability. So, I was stuck with that every Sunday, as well as on other holidays.

During the winter months, I carried a sickle and accompanied them to the paddy fields. We would cut sheaves of paddy and lay them on the ground to dry through the afternoon. Then, I dashed home, ran to the Hensanaga pond for a dip, sprinted back home, grabbed a bowl of pakhala, and then joined my buddies in going to school. On my return, I would again join Nana, Kaka and Bhaina in transporting bundles of dried paddy to the harvest area in our backyard. That exercise was strenuous, yet makes me feel nostalgic today. The sheaves were tied into bundles of paddy using a rope. Either Nana, Kaka or Bhaina helped place the bundles of paddy on my head, and then I was ready to make the trip. Each time I completed one trip and unloaded one lot, the head felt so light. A single load consisted of four to five bundles. If my share was to transport twenty bundles, it was my choice whether I made five trips with four bundles each, or four trips with five bundles. At night, when it was time to study, I was so tired that I would doze right from the beginning of the study hour. The number and frequency of whippings I received from Kaka for dozing in his tuition class is an amusing topic of discussion among my siblings, till date. After every single whack, I would wipe the sleep from my eyes a bit, see my fellow students laugh at me, stare at the same page for a while, and return to dozing again.

The primary school curriculum did not call for much effort. Whatever I could remember from just sitting in class was sufficient to get acceptable marks in exams. I had a great pal in Hemant. In the eyes of others, both of us were competing for the first position in class, but we felt happy for each other irrespective of who came first in the annual exam.

I remember, one day in our primary school, a meeting was held where it was decided that the teachers and students in the school would rehearse for a month to perform a musical drama, titled 'Lava Kusha'. A day later, Hemant and I were summoned for the roles of the twin sons of Rama and Sita. We also heard that both the roles called for singing talents. We looked at each other and chuckled. The school teachers apparently had noticed us sing Odia bhajans and folk songs together.

When I was in the seventh standard, Kaka got married and received a Philips radio in dowry. I listened to the radio more than Kaka or anyone else in the family. Gradually, my interest in singing increased. My earliest memory of singing a full song is an Odia bhajan, 'Prabhu pada tale pranati dhale'. I was sitting with many of my village friends in an evening Trinatha Mela. Gathering up the courage, I said, 'I also want to sing a bhajan. May I?' One of my childhood idols, Duna Mamu, was playing mridangam. 'Will you? Try, let's see,' he said, his voice encouraging. With folded hands and closed eyes, I began singing. All I could hear was my own voice in sync with Duna Mamu's mridangam. Upon completion of the song, when I opened my eyes, I saw that more people had gathered in the Trinatha Mela; a few hands patting my back and a few others tousling my hair, and most people saying a word or two of appreciation. I sang a bhajan; I was not sure of the blessings from the almighty, but I was sure of having received the blessings of several elders of my village. Going to bed that night, I realized that I had been subconsciously developing yet another hobby—singing.

One of my early inspirations in life was the famous Odia playback singer. Pranab Kishore Patnaik. His rendering of devotional and spiritual lyrics gave me goosebumps. He was my first idol outside my family. I began to imitate him. I developed a strong desire to meet him someday, but at that point, I had no idea how, when, or if, it would ever happen.

Later that year, both Hemant and I were selected by our upper primary school headmaster, Upendra sir, to appear for the Rural Talent Scholarship Exam. Students from several primary schools had travelled to the examination centre, Sundargram High School. Some twenty of us from nearby schools were accommodated in one big hall. There, I came across a girl. One thing about her particularly touched my heart; she was ever-smiling. I found myself thinking about her all the time. In rural Odisha then, it was almost a crime to talk to a girl of similar age, else I would have asked her this one question, 'how can you smile all the time?' I did not know what her real name was; everyone used to call her Bini. By the time we bid adieu to the exam venue, I had come to know through others that she was from Bilasuni upper primary school, and that she hailed from a zamindar family.

2

SELF-AWAKENING

AFTER THE SUMMER VACATION, ALL my primary schoolmates went to a high school that was relatively closer to our village. Following Bhaina's unsuccessful high school experience, right or wrong, Nana had developed a negative impression about that school. In his mind, therefore, he had decided to put me in a different high school, a bit farther away. So I had to walk four kilometres each way to Shri Gopaljew High School, Bilasuni.

Joining this school was not straightforward. The headmaster, Rajkishore Dash (fondly called Rajuna), was also my cousin, the elder son of my Pisi Nani (paternal aunt or bua). After my seventh-standard exams, during the summer vacations, when Nana first approached him, he asked me to meet him first. He tested my skills in math, and I was able to answer most of the oral arithmetic questions he volleyed at me. This won his approval, and he agreed to take me under his wing.

One of those questions still lingers in my mind: 'What is the significance of zero in an arithmetic operation?'

I did not follow the question. He understood my dilemma.

'What number would you get if you add or subtract zero from any number?' he clarified.

'The result would remain the same; zero does not add any value to an addition or subtraction operation,' I said. But I had understood the true import of the question, and thus continued: 'The same, however, is not true for multiplication. Any number when multiplied by zero would be reduced to zero itself.'

I saw a twinkle in Rajuna's eyes. 'What about division? What would you get if you divide any number by zero?' he probed.

I had no clue, but I thought it over, and took a chance. 'I do not know the exact answer, but I suppose any number divided by zero will turn out to be an immeasurably big number,' I said. Rajuna was ecstatic.

The simplicity of Rajuna's question was comprehensible, but its significance in real life was a mystery to me back then.

Rajuna was perceived by his siblings and cousins as a terror. I feared joining Bilasuni High School. But there was a silver lining. Bini was from Bilasuni upper primary school, and there was hope that she would probably be my batchmate, and that left me feeling ecstatic.

High school started off on an embarrassing note. On the very first day, Rajuna pinned me with his gaze. 'Dama, you are wearing a deep red shirt!' he exclaimed. Everyone looked at me and laughed. Cringing, I looked around, and realized that no one else was wearing a red shirt. 'Is it a crime to wear a red shirt?' I wondered internally. But Rajuna pronounced: 'You have to come to school wearing the school uniform. Until your uniform is procured, you can come in another coloured shirt, but not red.'

I had no option but to keep nodding my head. But on the way home, I was in a dilemma about what to wear the next day. The red shirt was the only one I owned! I knew that I would have to urge Nana to buy a school uniform, blue shorts and a white half-sleeved shirt, else I would not be allowed into school. I also knew that buying new clothes would take some time.

Saturday used to be a half-day in high school, and the last period was devoted to developing extracurricular skills among students—debating and singing being the most popular ones. One Saturday, Agadhu sir asked each one of us to sing a song. Since there weren't enough classrooms in school, a big hall was partitioned into three makeshift classrooms, using foldable mats that hung from bamboos spanning across the hall. The hall was basically an asbestos roof resting on four brick walls; the doors and windows were just openings on the walls with no panels. Therefore, whatever was being said in one class was audible in the others. When my turn came, I started singing my favourite Odia bhajan, 'Prabhu pada tale pranati dhale'. There was pin-drop silence in the hall. I was the first student that day to complete a full song. By the time I finished singing, all my batchmates were staring fixedly at me. Bini was looking at me too, with a quiet smile. Not just batchmates, a few teachers from other classes were also at the door, looking at me. I felt very shy, partly because I had never received such attention, but more so because I was wearing a shirt with torn sleeves, with buttons of different colours and sizes. Among the teachers who had come to the door was Banshidhar sir, who had an immense knowledge of music.

Later that day, I was asked to meet the headmaster, Rajuna, whom I had begun to fear. But that meeting was different. 'Your singing, especially the devotion in your voice, touched many hearts today,' he said, with compassion in his voice. Handing over a letter addressed to Nana, he continued, 'Dama, you can come to school in your red shirt till your school uniform is ready.' In the letter, he urged Nana to buy my school uniform as soon as possible. It was plausible that Banshidhar sir had met him, and apprised him about my singing, as well as the shirt I was wearing that day.

The prayer session in our high school was a grand affair. The students assembled on a field in front of the hall. The field itself was fenced with jasmine and other seasonal flowers and decorative plants. Students stood in five rows: all girls in the first, eighth-standard boys in the second, ninth-standard boys in the third, tenth-standard boys in the fourth and the eleventh-standard boys in the last row. Teachers stood in a row facing the students along the edge of the veranda. The lead singer, class-ten student Madan bhai, stood on the ground, in front of the teachers, between two beautiful croton plants. After prayers, Gopal bhai (Bini's elder brother) read out the news headlines, and Akshaya sir quizzed students on them.

One day, Madan bhai happened to be on leave, and Banshidhar sir called out my name to step in as lead singer. I had never ever stood in front of such a large crowd before, and all eyes were on me. I was initially nervous, but once the prayers began and everyone closed their eyes, it felt calming. Later during the day, I chuckled thinking that even if I had opened my eyes during prayers no one would have noticed; the teachers were behind me, and all the students facing me had their eyes closed anyway.

Commuting to Bilasuni High School took at least one hour each way. The monsoons came with many challenges, extending the commute time to three hours! While going to the Kantapada primary school, we had already experienced the slippery path along the canal. The narrow walkway through the paddy fields was manageable as well. But the challenge we faced while crossing over to the other side of the Marichia nali was quite unique. For about two months during the rainy season, everyone had to carry a towel in their bags, since the water level rose so high that for a stretch of about ten metres, one would need to swim. Girls were helped by adult male members, while boys would change into towels, fold the school uniform neatly and tuck it inside the bag, hold the bag high up above the water with one hand, and swim lopsidedly through the deeper stretch of the nali with the other. Once across, we would change back into our school uniforms and walk the remaining distance to school. The whole process would be repeated while returning.

During the first year in high school, my youngest sister Mitu was born. The court cases had also come to an end. Just when things appeared to have stabilized, something unexpected happened: Kaka announced his intention to set up his own household, separate from Nana. One kitchen got split into two. Not only the agricultural land and the betel farm, even the utensils and domestic animals were divided between Nana and Kaka. I vividly remember emotions running high in the family during this time, but could not do anything to prevent it. I was the most devastated, because I was most attached to Kaka, Maa and Khudi (aunt, Kaka's wife). As a child it was too painful for me.

But even after the separation, I continued to stay close to Kaka, Maa and Khudi, and of course, the Philips radio.

Kaka had abandoned the art of catching fish, but whenever I caught some fish, Bou and Sanjunani used to share the fish curry with Kaka and Khudi. The skill I had learnt from Kaka continued to preserve the symbolic link between the two kitchens.

My life was changing too; while all my primary schoolmates walked in one direction as a group to Kaliaghai, I would walk by myself in the opposite direction, to Bilasuni. Being alone, I was able to spend some quality time communicating with myself. A unique decision emerged from my ruminations, quite unconsciously.

In my formative years, I had been a spectator to a sequence of events over which I had no control. But now I realized the situation in my family wasn't unique in our village—many other families had similar circumstances. The concept of family planning did not exist, despite the families' acute scarcity of resources. Not many were trying to look at things any differently. I do not know exactly when I experienced a sense of awakening, nor did I know at that point what exactly I would do, but I was clear that I would follow a different path.

An early realization was that squabbling among siblings does not help anyone, it just makes everyone lose. I decided at a tender age that I would never ever initiate any action to split our joint family of three brothers.

Also, reflecting on what had happened to Kaka and Bhaina, I understood that there was not much benefit in adding labour to limited agricultural land; it was just adding more dependents to the same limited resource base. It dawned on me that the only way to combat scarcity was to stay close to books, pursue a job, and add to the family well-being with a complementary source of income. When I think back, I realize I differed from many of my childhood friends in one way—I never complained about my circumstances. I always had a smile on my face, even when my stomach was empty or even when I commuted to school in worn clothes.

Though the school schedule was exhausting, I continued to help Nana and Bhaina in paddy cultivation and betel farming. But at the same time, I began to take an interest in studies.

Until primary school, I had only one friend, Hemant, with whom I was competing. In high school, however, I was one among many. Students from at least five other primary schools had come to Bilasuni. Of these, I admired Manoj, who was witty and intelligent, and Bidyadhar, who was extremely industrious. Both were clearly ahead of me. I came fifth in my first exam in high school, but by the end of that academic year, with determination and hard work,

I moved to the third position. This progression helped boost my self-confidence; I saw a ray of hope.

It wasn't just the external environs my brain was responding to; I found myself on a journey into my inner self too. I had a habit of dozing in the evening while immersed in studies, and the tiring commute to my new school compounded the problem. Bou came up with a solution—she told me to close the book, finish supper and go to sleep, and that she would wake me up early in the morning, when I would be refreshed and could study for a few hours before going to school. That worked well.

As I entered my teens, I experienced the natural biological changes in my body and mind. I began to like 'secret conversations' about girls, and began taking interest in borrowing and reading books with explicit content. One evening, I was reading one such book with full concentration, well past 9 p.m. When Sanjunani came to call me for supper, I answered that I was reading something very important, and that it would take some more time. She served supper to the others and finished her own. But Bou and Nana waited patiently so that I could complete my studies for the day before the three of us ate together. Both chatted about some household matters while I remained glued to the book. They thought I was reading something extremely important, whereas in reality, I was reading a cheap novel.

However, a feeling of guilt kicked in, making me miserable. 'My parents are not educated enough to check over my shoulder whether I am reading a reference book, or a story book, or a cheap novel,' I thought. 'Their love for me makes them trust me completely, and their ignorance forces no checks on me. Is this the way I am going to exploit their blind trust?'

That was the moment when the true meaning of the adage 'character is what you do when no one is watching you' sunk in. A few tears trickled down my face as I closed the book and asked for supper. That moment taught me to choose the path that appeared tough and monotonous, but was the right one nevertheless, over one that held a temporary charm. The next day, I returned the book to the friend I had borrowed it from, and never went back to reading cheap novels again.

It is not that I did not have the natural instincts of a teenager. Looking directly at a schoolmate of the opposite gender and a similar age was not customary, but on days when I was called upon to fill in the role of the lead singer in our prayer class, I did take my chances to look at Bini occasionally. I also took part with friends in all kinds of naughty conversations in school, but spending a lot of time on anything beyond academics or household chores was just out of the question. I trained myself not to repress my instinct, but to redirect it to follow my conscience.

At this juncture, I derived constant inspiration from one of the respected elders in our village: Bijoy Mamu. He was among the tallest and most handsome young men, the best football and kabaddi player, and acted as the hero each time a drama was staged in our village. As a student, he was the first from our village to secure a first class in the high school board exam, and had gone on to complete his graduation. Yet, he was unemployed. The reason I admired him was that despite his all-round talent and the fact that he came from the richest family in our village at the time, he had no qualms about going to the paddy fields and joining the workers in farming. 'If one is not employed, it does not mean he should sit idle in anticipation of a job and stop leading a respectful life,' he would say, and exemplify it with his behaviour.

I was sure he would get employed one day; that it was just a matter of time. And that thought was comforting.

3

CALL OF THE GURUKUL

WHEN I WAS IN THE ninth standard, the residential quarters for the headmaster were completed, and Rajuna's family moved into the school campus. I was summoned to join his family as a resident.

The thought of living in close proximity with Rajuna gave me chills, but it was an opportunity of a lifetime, and I knew it. I packed my books, notepads and geometry box in a trunk, while Sanjunani packed the few clothes I had. The trunk was rather too big for its contents. I gave a smile as Sanjunani closed the trunk.

'Study well,' Bou and Sanjunani wished me. Bhaina helped me lift the trunk onto my head. Nana carried a bag of rice and I had the trunk on my head as we walked past our village danda. Little did I know that the trunk would become my most valuable companion for many years to come, and that walk would turn out to be the beginning of the defining moments of my life.

I had been commuting to Bilasuni High School for over a year but had not realized the discipline followed inside the campus until I started living there. A day in the hostel began with a dip in the

Board Pokhari (pond), followed by morning prayer. Both rituals had to be completed before sunrise. Defaulters faced punishment—they were forced to kneel and stay that way for fifteen minutes. There was a bell for all important checkpoints of the day—waking up, morning assembly, evening prayers and mealtimes. About half an hour every evening was devoted to a football game or some sort of physical exercise. Apart from me, Rajuna's youngest brother Paina (whom I called Paina Nana, shortened to Paiana, out of respect) also lived in the quarters. Both Paiana and I learnt to be disciplined by participating in the rituals followed by the hostel residents.

The initial weeks were filled with mixed emotions. On one hand, I was missing Bou, Sanjunani, Bhaina, Kaka, Khudi and Maa, and on the other, I was beginning to appreciate the discipline in school. I felt a new chapter of my life had just begun.

Rajuna's wife, Mani Bhauja, was by far the best cook I had come across. There was magic in her cooking, though that feeling was partly because I was not used to eating such good-quality meals at home. Every meal served by her felt like a feast.

Back at home, both Bhaina and Sanjunani got married on the same day, so as we welcomed my sister-in-law (Nuabou) into the family, we also lost our dearest member, Sanjunani, to her new home. The net addition to the home was zero, but there was significant expenditure involved in conducting the weddings. We were staring at acute scarcity.

Bhaina was extremely hardworking, no doubt, but getting married to Nuabou fired him up, motivating him to increase his responsibility in running the home.

Nuabou turned out to be a wonderful surprise. She was the perfect addition to the family, and with her caring nature, love and affection, she never let any of us feel the absence of Sanjunani.

A few months into their marriage, I recall Bhaina and Nuabou taking this bold stand together: 'Let us completely eliminate any discretionary expenses, cut down or postpone even some mandatory ones; let us also resolve to pay off any pending loans, and never borrow money again to cover our regular expenses.' Nana and Bou both had smiles on their faces, recognizing their daughter-in-law as the much-needed addition to the family.

To pay my boarding charges, Nana had volunteered to provide twenty kilograms of rice every month to Rajuna. That was what Nana carried with him the day I left the village with my trunk. For subsequent instalments, I had to visit my village once a month. Walking four kilometres carrying a twenty-kilogram rice bag on my head was a herculean task, because my own body weight was a little over thirty kilos at the time! Each time I visited home, I felt happy. I used to stay over for the weekend. Nuabou had brought with her a different vibe—a wind of change, a breath of fresh air.

In school, Rajuna was perceived as a terror. He was principled, and a disciplinarian. Whenever he handed out a punishment to a student, it was extreme. Whoever faced his wrath once did not forget it for a long time. Paiana and I experienced it once. Being of similar age, we used to engage in mischief and squabbles all the time. Paiana was one year older than me. Therefore, I was invariably at the receiving end. This incident took place on a Sunday afternoon, when annual exams were around the corner. Instead of studying, we were locked in a serious fight. Rajuna noticed it and meted out heavy punishment to both of us—basically a sound whipping using a seasoned cane.

In the evening, while we were crying on each other's shoulders, a terrible idea struck me. Early in the morning, before anyone was awake, I wrote a revolting note on a slip of paper, placed it underneath the doormat and fled from Rajuna's quarters. Upon reaching my home in the village, I got the shock of my life. 'You were sent to school to save time on your daily commute so that you could devote more time to studying. Looks like you are spending more time squabbling instead! Go back to school, else I will put a full stop to your studies. You could then join us in farming full time,' said Nana, his warning sounding more frightening than Rajuna's whipping. I had no option but to run back to school.

By the time I reached school, the note under the doormat had already been uncovered. Not sure how the message had spread but Pisa, Rajuna's father, had also arrived. I stayed away from Rajuna, hiding the whole day in some classroom. When I returned to the quarters in the evening, I overheard this argument between Pisa and Rajuna.

'You must not allow Dama to get close to Paina. He has been a bad influence on him,' Pisa said.

'Why have you come to that conclusion, Bapa?' Rajuna asked.

'Since Dama arrived in your quarters, Paina's marks are going south,' replied Pisa.

'Paina is a year older than Dama. He should be in a position to influence Dama positively instead of getting influenced by him negatively,' said Rajuna.

'That is not easy as both are of similar age. Their minds will collaborate on the wrong things,' Pisa said.

'Are you advising me to instruct Dama and Paina to behave like strangers, Bapa? They are cousins living under the same roof!' Rajuna protested.

'I do not want to argue with you. If you can't do that, then you send Dama back home. Else, I will take Paina back with me and have him commute from our village to school daily as he was doing earlier,' Pisa warned.

But Rajuna was adamant. 'Paina is my own brother and Dama is my cousin. However, I am convinced that Dama is not a negative influence on Paina. By taking the side of my own brother against a cousin, I cannot do injustice to Dama. Pardon me. I will try to work on both, but if you are still adamant about your decision, you may choose to take Paina away from here. Dama is staying.'

It was difficult to hide the tears rolling down my face. 'Rajuna, save me. Give me just one chance!' I prayed, as Pisa was gradually softening his stance towards me. At the same time, a strong resolution of sorts was building within me.

Pisa himself was a fatherly figure to me and was a great person, there was no doubt about that in my mind. It is just that when one had to choose between a son and a nephew, most people would choose the former. But then there are a few others who exemplify a god-like demeanour, like Rajuna. He chose fairness and justice over yielding to his father's personal urge.

I was eventually forgiven, and continued to live in the company of Rajuna, Bhauja and their four little children, and of course, Paiana. I adopted Rajuna's quarters as my first home for the next two years.

Mani Bhauja managed all the household chores singlehandedly. She needed to draw around thirty buckets of water daily from the thirty foot-deep open well inside the campus, and I noticed she had been struggling. So, Paiana and I stepped in. Paiana, however, was approaching his final year in high school, and needed more study time. I, therefore, spared him from the routine of drawing water and took over that responsibility entirely. That not only helped me get my daily dose of exercise, but also resulted in winning an extra share of Mani Bhauja's love. Those two years in Rajuna's quarters would stand out for developing self-discipline and building character.

After that infamous Sunday afternoon, Paiana and I were hardly seen squabbling anymore. Paiana was the undisputed topper of his batch, and being a year junior, I always looked up to him and tried to emulate him. While it is true that I was still at the receiving end during his moments of rare aggression, it is also true that I was the recipient of his selfless love and mentoring. I was inspired by his neat handwriting. I do not recall a single instance when he refused to clarify my doubts citing his own studies. Because of the proximity and his willingness to help, I used to interrupt him and frequently run to him to clarify my doubts, especially in mathematics. I vividly remember that moment when I approached him for a deduction problem in geometry one day. 'Think Dama, apply your own mind before running to me for help. You can solve this problem by yourself if you try hard enough. After a few months I will be gone. Then who will you run to with your doubts?' His voice was compassionate and reprimanding at the same time. My approach to difficult problems in life changed from that moment, especially in academics. Since then, I consciously practiced pushing myself to limits before seeking external help.

The hostel superintendent, Akshaya sir, persuaded the residents of our school hostel to engage in gardening. Apart from developing a productive hobby, the fresh produce from the garden was used in the hostel mess, thereby helping reduce the boarding charges of the residents. Exhibiting competitive spirit, I also tilled a piece of land in front of Rajuna's quarters and planted a few seasonal vegetables. Working with Bou, I had prior experience in vegetable farming. It was heartening to see the garden flourishing under my singular effort, yielding more produce than the combined produce of all the other residents of the hostel.

That year, there was a surplus yield of bhindi (okra) and tomatoes in the garden. 'Dama, why don't you pluck and deliver a bag of okra and tomatoes to the secretary's home?' Rajuna asked one Sunday afternoon. Bini's father was the secretary of our school's management committee. I was ecstatic; I fancied a chance to see Bini that day!

Since the day I was forgiven by Rajuna, I had pledged to be his unconditional disciple. I began to pay utmost attention to his teachings.

He had a unique way of conveying difficult messages. One day, Manoj could not answer a relatively simple question. Rajuna was convinced that Manoj was the most intelligent boy in our class, but not as hardworking.

'What is ten multiplied by zero, Manoj?' he asked.

'Zero,' Manoj answered.

'Similarly, even though one is super intelligent or "ten out of ten", if effort is zero, the output is zero,' said Rajuna.

With one simple analogy, Rajuna had motivated Manoj—he had acknowledged his intelligence, and drilled into him the importance of hard work. Manoj had a smile on his face as he internalized the message; I chuckled too, recalling Rajuna's question before admitting me to Bilasuni High School on the significance of 'zero' in arithmetic operations.

Another day, he shared this piece of wisdom in class: 'The best way to remember and retain information is to review class notes on the very same evening that the topic has been covered in class.' I followed his advice and reaped instant benefits. It helped retain knowledge and enhanced my personal productivity. He himself was enthused when he noticed me following his words. He then inspired me to take the next step by saying, 'The best way to get the most out of a class is to glance over, in the morning, the topics that are likely to be covered on that particular day.' As I followed his advice, not only did I find myself better prepared to answer the questions asked by the teachers, I also could ask better questions.

This practice of reviewing the day's topics the same evening, as well as looking up in the morning the topics to be covered that day, soon became a habit that has stood the test of time. Not only did it help me in school and college, but also stayed with me throughout my professional career. I take a few minutes every evening reflecting on the things that happened during the workday, and the following morning, spend some time reviewing my position and preparedness over the topics and issues that would most likely come up throughout the day.

Patterns etched into our brain and muscle memory become second nature. Once a habit is fully internalized, action follows automatically, and thus consumes a lot less physical and mental energy. Rajuna had unparalleled influence in my development as a practitioner of good habits. In a short time, he had imbibed in me the habit of waking up early, the significance of hard work, the benefit of staying up to date with my studies, and the ability to proactively handle anticipated challenges.

After my ninth standard annual exam, during the summer break, our village boys were staging a play. I was the unanimous choice for the role of a child actor. Nana, however, was dead set against me acting in the play. He had been receiving encouraging feedback from Rajuna about my progress in studies, and wanted me to capitalize on that momentum and do even better. For him it was simple: he wanted to see me with books as often as possible. Anything else, to him, appeared a distraction. So, he reprimanded me. The rehearsals were held at night. After finishing my studies, I ate supper and went to the rehearsal without Nana's knowledge. He did notice me sleeping for most of the next day. Becoming suspicious, he made me sleep next to him one night. I pretended to fall asleep. As soon as I heard him snore, I quietly opened the door and joined the rehearsal in our village club house. After a few hours, the inevitable happened. A resounding slap landed on my back when I was immersed in delivering a passionate dialogue. That brought an abrupt end to the rehearsal. The senior boys, especially Bijay Mamu, pleaded with Nana to permit me to act in the play. But Nana was adamant. I was not there to witness the argument as I was afraid of receiving more punishment from Nana, and had run back to the same room from where I had vanished just a few hours back. To my surprise, Nana did not mete out any more punishment. Just one line: 'As soon as you wake up in the morning, you are going back to school.' The verdict was irreversible.

I had been looking forward to acting in the play as a way to unwind during the summer vacations and then take up my studies with renewed momentum from the beginning of the upcoming academic year. But that was not going to happen. I chose not to utter a single word of protest to Nana. The incident made its way to Rajuna. 'Acting, like singing or sketching, is a form of art. It is an extracurricular skill that helps in the all-round development of a young child,' said Rajuna, and his wisdom was eventually successful in enriching Nana's outlook. On my part, however, I observed restraint. 'There is plenty of time ahead of me for my all-round development, and there is no point in hurting Nana's sentiments now,' I told myself.

In the tenth standard, there came a chance to go on a two-week-long National Cadet Corps camp in Chandikhol, a beautiful tourist location a few kilometres away from Cuttack. Apart from participating in parades and shooting exercises during the day, the camp was supposed to offer an opportunity to showcase extracurricular skills in acting and singing. I was not great at parades or shooting, but was picked by our NCC teacher, Charan sir, to be on our school team, mainly because of my singing talent. But I had different plans. I attended the camp, but bunked most of the parade sessions to hide and study. I was hauled up for missing the parade sessions, but I remained unperturbed. My singular focus on academics had already set in. Upon return from the NCC camp, we had to appear in the half-yearly exam. For the first time, I wasn't third; I topped.

Looking back, I am convinced beyond any doubt that one factor helped me focus on academics: lack of access to money. Lodging was in Rajuna's quarters. Whatever charges I was supposed to contribute towards boarding were covered through the supply of homegrown rice. The tuition fee was subsidized for students who did relatively well in class. Books were borrowed from the school's book bank. A geometry box, once procured, was an asset for the rest of high school. Therefore, I did not have any grounds to ask anyone for money. There was no concept of 'pocket money' for me. The only sundry expenses I can recall were for buying notebooks, pens and pencils. I rarely used to buy soap, but trust me, I never stole any after the Ganesh puja incident. I used Paiana's soap occasionally, and after he left for college, I managed by getting hold of the residual soaps in Rajuna's quarters. Bathing with soap was not a necessity as such. Washing clothes was not a big problem; I did not have many clothes anyway.

Talking of clothes, I had never worn briefs till I completed the tenth standard. I recall a funny incident. Paiana had just received the results of his high school board exam and was applying to colleges. While he cleared his book rack, I was busy grabbing his old books, test papers, notebooks, pens and pencils. During the concurrent exercise of discarding and inheriting, I found a pair of briefs. Paiana did not notice; I just grabbed them and tried them on. What can I say? It felt intriguingly odd.

I had never let scarcity weigh down my state of mind, and lived my teen years just like another teenager. Despite the fear of Rajuna's punishment, I used to indulge in petty mischief. I assessed well, and only indulged in mischief that could at best result in some scolding or mild punishment. These would break the monotony of routine, and give me some much-needed entertainment without the risk of being thrown out of the quarters.

One Sunday, we were taking an afternoon nap after a heavy midday meal. I wonder now about how we slept comfortably on benches that were barely nine inches wide; if you just attempted to turn a little, you would tumble over and land with a thud. That afternoon, we saw a batchmate of ours, Kailash, sleeping on his back, on a bench. We were keenly observing how his chest was rising and falling with each breath. My eyes fell on a pile of bricks stacked at the rear of the classroom. That is when a playful idea struck me. I took one brick and placed it on Kailash's chest. We were intrigued, observing how a full brick was also rising and falling in sync with his breathing. I then added a second brick. But Kailash still did not wake up. We began giggling. Pandit sir happened to be passing by. Without us noticing, he peeped into the classroom to see what was going on and caught me red-handed while I was placing yet another brick on Kailash's chest. He started rebuking us all. Promptly we began to disperse from the scene. 'At least remove those bricks from his chest,' shouted Pandit sir. I removed the bricks obediently. But Kailash remained asleep!

On another day, my friend Sudhir and I entered one of the hostel rooms and locked ourselves from inside. The last period of the day was gardening, which we had conspired to bunk. We gossiped about secret teenaged stuff while the rest of our batchmates toiled in the school garden. Everything was fine until I needed to go to the urinal. It was then that I recalled that during recess, we had a water-drinking competition, and I had emptied an entire big jug. 'Do not open the door at this point; if you do both of us will get caught,' Sudhir warned. I was in a fix. My eyes fell on two empty kerosene bottles, both quite small. In no time, both got filled, but I was not even half done. I then peed into a few lanterns, feeling the relief of a lifetime. Sudhir was in splits seeing me screwing the lids back on to the lanterns and bottles. When the gardening class got over, we opened the door and took a quick peek. The gardening teacher had already left. Sudhir and I joined the rest as if we had been part of the group all along.

As the evening study bell rang, our hostel mates were ecstatic, thinking that someone had filled their bottles and lanterns with kerosene, by mistake. Their joy, of course, was short-lived as they soon discovered that their lanterns malfunctioned. There was a massive hunt for the culprit. Sudhir and I would not open our mouths; instead, we joined the team of friends hunting for the culprit. But the truth did get out, and I received heavy thrashing at the hands of Rajuna. The next few days in school were embarrassing; everyone, including the teachers, kept staring at me, laughing.

Here's another mischief I genuinely regretted for a long time. During the annual sports day event that year, I had some arguments with Agadhu sir, our physical training instructor. I could not influence his decision beyond a point, and was irritated. When it got dark, I deflated his bicycle tyres. I also unscrewed his bell and flung it into an adjacent pond. I had no idea what came over me; I did not throw away the bolt and the nut. Instead, I hid them in my pocket. Later in the evening, when Agadhu sir noticed the condition of his bicycle, he came to Rajuna, suspecting me. Rajuna was known for being fair. 'What makes you believe that Dama could be behind this mischief?' Agadhu sir referred to the argument I had had with him earlier. Unlike the lantern incident, there was no evidence against me this time around. There was no Sudhir, or anyone else, as witness. I had indulged in mischief all alone. Rajuna had no history of punishing anyone without evidence. I could have refuted the charges. I looked at Agadhu sir. There was no trace of vindictiveness. There was only helplessness on his pious face. My conscience was killing me. With regret, I hung my head in shame and surrendered.

'Where have you hidden the bell?' probed Rajuna.

'Threw it into the pond,' I said, nervously.

'Go find it. Do not come out of the pond until you find it.'

There I was, hoping to find a bell that I had thrown into the pond myself. Fortunately, I had been a bit mindful while flinging it, so I didn't have to search the entire pond. I combed through the pond bed with my feet, and having located it, took a dip in the neck-deep water, sank to the bottom, and gripped it.

It was the last working day before school closed for Christmas holidays, and around nine o'clock at night. Not just Rajuna and Agadhu sir, many of my schoolmates were witnessing the event like a funfair. Everyone was wearing a shirt; some even had a sweater on. I was shivering in wet pants.

I handed over the bell to Agadhu sir. Then I reached into the pocket of my damp pants while everyone stared curiously at me. Though I still looked down in shame, I couldn't resist chuckling as I took out the nut and the bolt from my pocket and held it out towards Agadhu sir. Everyone cracked up, including Rajuna and Agadhu sir.

There was no fixed pattern to my mischief, nor was there a fixed pattern to Rajuna's reaction. He knew exactly what form of punishment would stick; I would have preferred whipping over entering a pond on a wintry night.

As my tenth standard annual exams ended, Rajuna was visiting Cuttack to receive the school staff's salaries. After an early supper, I succeeded in persuading twelve of my batchmates to sneak out from the hostel on bicycles. We went to watch the night show of an Odia movie in Niali, a small town around eight kilometres away from our school. The movie ended at midnight. Instead of returning to the school hostel, we dared to pedal away another forty kilometres to Konark. There was ample time. We took a nap under the lighthouse for an hour or so, watched the spectacular sunrise along the east coast road, circled around the Sun Temple for a little while before starting the ride back, aiming to reach school by early afternoon.

Our initial plan was only the movie; Konark was an impromptu idea. By the time we were ready to bid farewell to Konark, we were already tired and hungry. Pedalling forty kilometres back to school felt like a daunting task. Upon carefully checking each other's pockets, we discovered just a few coins. This incident took place in 1978; a few twenty-five-paisa, ten-paisa and five-paisa coins held tremendous value. With those coins we managed to order a small quantity of breakfast. Portions were proportional to one's contribution to the coin pool, which meant I got almost nothing. Thus, the return journey was not as exciting as the one going out. To make matters worse, the anxiety of heavy punishment upon reaching school began to grip me, as I was the mastermind. Add to this, three of the twelve bicycles, including the one I was riding, were 'borrowed' from friends without their knowledge. The thought of all these facts reaching the hostel superintendent were ominously hanging over our heads. So much so that my feet turned leaden, and I just could not pedal the last ten kilometres. I asked my friends to carry on and forced myself to rest under a tree.

By the time I reached Niali, it was half past one in the afternoon. I parked the bicycle in front of a sweet shop, and sat on a bench without saying a word. The shopkeeper looked at me. After a few minutes he asked, 'Want to eat something?' I wanted to nod my head, but could only end up saying, 'I don't have any money'. After a few minutes of silence, the man continued probing, 'Where did you come from?'

I couldn't hide anything further, and narrated the whole story. I expected a rebuke. On the contrary, I saw him serving two rasagollas on a small plate. My eyes lit up. As soon as he placed the plate in front of me, I gobbled them up in no time, drank a glass of water, and vanished from the shop. I'm not sure whether I thanked him before leaving.

When I reached the school, I learnt that my other friends had already confessed to Rajuna that it was my game plan, and that he was waiting for me to arrive!

There was silence all over. I wanted the day to pass somehow. As usual, I joined everyone for the evening prayer session. Those of us who had been to Konark were asked not to disperse after the prayer. 'Bad time ahead,' we thought. As the leader of the gang, I thought I was finished.

'Which movie did you all watch?' asked Rajuna.

'Krishna Sudama,' one of us said.

'That must have been a beautiful movie!'

At that point it was difficult to judge whether he was sarcastic.

'One by one, can all of you tell me one thing that you learned from watching the movie?'

Everyone said something, one by one, as I pondered over my take on the movie.

'I was moved to tears noticing Krishna's love and admiration for his poor childhood friend Sudama. No matter how much I grow in life, I will never ever ignore a childhood friend of mine. This is what I learned from the movie,' I said when it was my turn.

It was probably this answer that saved all of us that day.

'Your annual exam has just gotten over. It is therefore acceptable for you to go for a movie. But you should have informed the hostel superintendent about your plan. Not doing that was your mistake. He was certainly worried about all of you. Extending your adventure to Konark was another mistake. But that is all behind you now. You seem to have learned great lessons from the movie. So, you are excused this one time,' said Rajuna.

While his reactions to situations were unpredictable, no one ever doubted Rajuna's intentions. Whenever he meted out heavy punishment, it felt hard, but a few moments later, it also felt fair. Whenever he forgave, it felt like a close shave, and also meant that repeating that mistake would have grave consequences.

After supper that night, I could not fall asleep, even though I was completely exhausted. I reflected on my situation—where I was, how far I had come, my journey. Considering what had happened in the case of Kaka and Bhaina, my parents did not expect big things from me. Till then, I hadn't dreamt too big either. 'Somehow if I study well and just about manage to become a school teacher, life will be beautiful,' I had thought. I don't believe that becoming a school teacher is any small accomplishment. Rajuna was, and continues to be, my number one idol, and he was a school teacher. It is just that becoming a school teacher out of passion and noble intention, like Rajuna, is one thing and becoming a school teacher because one feels one can do no better is another altogether. To add to it, I had an imaginary ceiling over my head. No one in the entire Padhi community in my village had even passed matriculation. I had no big benchmark to follow. My only conscious attempt was to beat my own past performance, each time I faced a new exam. I was my own benchmark. That had worked for me. As I progressed through the first three years of high school, I saw myself gradually moving from fifth to first. I was competing with myself all along, and I had overtaken many of my batchmates along the way without any feeling of rivalry. This realization became a life lesson for me.

I began to draw inspiration from my own journey.

There is no harm in aspiring for something bigger in life. I dared to dream, and I promised myself I would try harder. With those thoughts, I gradually drifted off to sleep.

Waking up the next morning, I requested Rajuna if I could stay in the quarters through the summer vacations instead of going to my village. Seeing my motivation, Rajuna felt happy. By that time, I had already turned into Mani Bhauja's pet. She felt happy too.

So, no Raja Festival that summer, and no kite-flying. No singing of bhajans in the evening Trinatha Mela. No mischief in the company of my village pals. And no extra helping hand for Nana and Bhaina in paddy fields and betel farming.

The syllabus for the Odisha State High School Certificate Board Examination was brutal. It spanned across all the topics covered in the ninth to eleventh standards. Mathematics and English accounted for 200 each of the total 800 marks. Mathematics was hard, but at least felt logically built over the topics covered during the previous years. English was the hardest. There were thirty poems, ten in each year. There was one question, worth twenty marks, to write the summary of one poem out of two given choices.

So, essentially, one had to prepare for twenty-nine of the thirty poems to be assured of answering that one question.

Having studied in an Odia-medium school, I did not have the ability to read, comprehend and write the summary of a poem in English all on my own. But there were books and test papers, and some scribbled class notes from prior years. Patiently, I referred to all the sources, compiled them, and neatly wrote down a one-page summary for the first poem. It was then time to mug up. I found that I had a talent for it; I had plenty of unused brain. To be sure that I had mugged up correctly, I wrote it down and then compared word-by-word with my notebook. Any mistake I found, and it was back to mugging up. On day two, I repeated the process for the second poem, and made it a point to revise the first poem again. Gradually over the next ten days, I had not only memorized the one-page summaries of all twenty poems that were covered in the ninth and tenth standards, but also found the recipe to tackle the remaining ten that were supposed to be covered during the upcoming year.

I applied the same formula to the other essay-type questions in English.

An important journey had just begun, that of sheer hard work.

Rajuna was our mathematics teacher. That was enough for me to pay special attention to that subject. We had two papers in maths, worth a hundred marks each. I had not crossed the ninety marks barrier in either paper until the class ten annual exam. The goal was to get as close to a hundred as possible in both the papers. No one in our school had achieved the feat of scoring two hundred in mathematics yet. Dharani bhai had been the closest two years prior; he had scored ninety-nine and ninety-eight. In aggregate, three short of the magic number.

I began taking a crack at two sample mathematics model papers every single day. The morning started with a model paper from Compulsory Mathematics; afternoons were for compilation and mugging of English essay-type questions, and in the evening, it was one model paper of Optional Mathematics. Rajuna helped in clarifying doubts, but it always felt scary to go to him voluntarily. He had very little tolerance for silly mistakes. That worked in its own way. Unknowingly, another good habit had started developing within me: I was taking responsibility and trying hard to solve the difficult problems myself, and checking my own work thoroughly before asking for help—a learning that Paiana had instilled in me a year ago.

Before the end of the summer vacations, I had developed much-needed confidence in the most difficult thing—the essay-type questions in English. In addition, I had not only reviewed the entire mathematics syllabus of the ninth and tenth standards, but also got a preview of the chapters likely to be covered in the eleventh.

Apart from English and mathematics, there were four other subjects: Odia, Science, Social Studies and Sanskrit. It was difficult to fail in Odia, yet it was impossible to score very high marks even if one devoted a lot of time to it. So, I gave it just as much focus as it deserved. Social Studies was interesting: History felt like reading story books, and Geography felt logical. None of them felt threatening, so I took it easy. Science felt logical and lively, and I found myself to be good at it. Fortunately, we had excellent teachers for Science too. Pradipta sir had a unique style of teaching: I vividly remember how he poked his own thumb with a safety pin in the class to demonstrate the phenomenon of blood clotting!

The only subject I didn't have a strategy for was Sanskrit; it gave me jitters. I knew that it would not be of much use to me later, so all I needed was to secure a pass in this subject. I had never failed in it before, but I was far from feeling confident.

While introspecting about different subjects, I realized one thing: English would be important irrespective of what I chose to do in future. I could not afford to take it lightly. Mugging up essay-type questions and scoring some marks was probably an acceptable option back then, but English as a subject needed more attention.

So, I began to spend significant amounts of time on an English grammar book, and an Odia-to-English translation book. Jyotshna Madam was available to help. My strategy paid rich dividends, as I was able to enhance my vocabulary and could also begin to make sense of what I was mugging up. It also helped when I was unable to recall what I had mugged up. I was able to frame at least small sentences.

I realized life offered no shortcuts—there was a lot of hard work ahead.

The first three months of the eleventh standard just flew by. In the first preparatory exam, I did well in every subject, except Sanskrit. To pass, one needed thirty marks; I was only seven higher than that. Pandit sir, our Sanskrit teacher, cautioned, 'You are on the borderline. If you fail in Sanskrit, you will fail the board exam. You may come first among your batchmates, Dama, but what is the use?'

My situation was not very different from that of Bhaina, who had failed his board exam for want of marks in just one subject.

I was aware of my situation. I was probably waiting for a wake-up call, and it had arrived.

Over the next two months, Sanskrit consumed most of my time. One does not have to overthink in a language; in English, for example, it is futile to ask why 'but' and 'put' don't rhyme while 'bat' and 'pat' do. But Sanskrit gave me even more trouble. In every other language I am aware of, there are only two forms of nouns, singular and plural. Sanskrit has three: singular, dual (dwivachanam) and plural. To add to the complexity, the languages I was then familiar with had two genders, male and female. Sanskrit has three: male, female, and neuter (napunsakling). Beyond a point, I just stopped worrying, and instead, began applying my own proven formula: mugging up. Beginning with 'nara' and 'path', I began rote-learning one 'shabd roop' (noun form) and one 'dhatu roop' (verb form) every day. Odia-to-Sanskrit translation accounted for twenty marks, so I began translating small sentences. I found a give-and-take partner in Kailash (who had fortunately not taken the incident of me placing a stack of bricks on his chest seriously). I helped him in mathematics; he helped clarify my doubts in Sanskrit.

When I paid attention, comprehending a story or poem in Sanskrit and translating its essence to Odia was not all that difficult. Unlike English, the stories in Sanskrit were native to India—many of them from mythology, which, thanks to my mother, I had liked since childhood.

After two months of meticulous effort, I began to feel comfortable in Sanskrit.

On Independence Day that year, a debate competition was held in our school. I had never attempted using my oratory skills earlier. As a child artiste, in primary school and in my village, and as the lead singer in high school prayer class, I had overcome stage fear to some extent. I became curious about debate.

In previous years, I had observed that the formula for winning debate competitions was straightforward: long sentences delivered with passion, and without pause. Once you delivered a long sentence, the audience started clapping, and it hardly mattered what you were saying. At this point, the speaker ought not to slow down or wait for the applause to stop; one must raise the decibel level and continue. The winner would be the one who drew the biggest applause.

I compiled a page on the topic given for the debate, thinking it was yet another essay-type question. By then a master of mugging up, I memorized the entire page and practiced a few times, standing in front of empty benches and desks, to make sure that I could recollect the long sentences one after the other without long pauses.

The formula worked. I came first, and stunned Rashmi, who used to win most of our school debate competitions. If someone was happier than me, it was Rajuna, and the English teacher, Jyotshna Madam. But that was the first and last debate I ever participated in; I thought it was a lot of work. I did not know what I would do in my career, but I thought I had more important things to do than standing in front of a crowd and eliciting cheers. I got back to studies.

By the time I appeared for the second and final preparatory exam in the eleventh standard, I had devised my own strategy for every subject: a combination of thinking, practicing, relating and smart guessing, and rote learning. Literature and language subjects no longer felt intimidating; preparation for social studies appeared adequate. Mathematics and science felt fun and worth exploring more.

The results of the final preparatory exam were a confidence boost: I was beginning to feel that I could aspire for admission to a good college. It was time to take the final leap.

Aiming to get as close to two hundred as possible in mathematics, I continued the habit of solving two model question papers daily. It was getting boring, but I could solve familiar problems faster, thereby making more time to solve unfamiliar ones. As the board exam drew close, I was hardly encountering unfamiliar problems. 'Practice makes perfect', and I was experiencing it.

For science, my strategy was different. There were five long questions, worth sixteen marks each, totalling up to eighty out of hundred. Even if they were not subjective questions, it was impossible to get more than twelve in each of those five questions. So even if one got all the remaining twenty marks in objective type questions, the highest one could aspire for in science was eighty out of hundred. It was imperative to prepare as-close-to-perfect answers as I could to the five long questions. That introduced another level of discipline to my preparation for the board exam, the pursuit of excellence.

I followed the same discipline to improve my confidence in social studies and Odia as well: one after another, I compiled the answers to several possible subjective questions, read them multiple times, and attempted to write them down. That was the best way to introduce as much objectivity as possible into subjective questions.

The habit of writing gave me other significant benefits—for one, my handwriting improved a lot. Filling up the empty pages of notebooks collected from Paiana also gave me a lot of happiness. Most importantly, I could stretch my study hours during the night; I was not falling asleep as easily while writing as I used to when engaged in plain reading.

Every gratifying journey ends on an emotional note. 'Will you visit us after you graduate and join college, Dama?' Mani Bhauja asked once, a few days before the board exam. I knew she would miss me the most. I had also not got any significant punishment from Rajuna during the entire final year. He would not say it openly, but I knew he was happy with the effort I had put in and the progress I had made.

To add to my emotions, Rajuna got me a surprise gift: full pants and a shirt. To me, it meant a lot. He bought the fabric but it had to be stitched, and he knew I did not have money for that, so he paid for it. He also knew that I could not be barefoot while wearing full pants so, thoughtfully, he had bought a pair of chappals as well. That was the first time I ever wore footwear. Now, the funniest part: I had heard from friends that it was odd to wear full pants without underwear. But the one I had snatched from Paiana a year ago was long gone, and I could not ask Rajuna.

The dates for the final exams were announced, and the centre was Kasarda High School.

I had to visit my home in the village before I proceeded to the exam venue, and I hadn't been there in two months. Most importantly, I needed some money; I had to buy one pair of underwear at least.

Nana, Kaka and Bhaina enquired about my preparations for the exams. Bou, Khudi and Maa had begun offering diyas (traditional lamps) to Grameswara Mahadeva. 'God will listen to our prayers; you will bring laurels to our family,' added Nuabou, raising expectations while showering blessings. I collected my money and headed back to school.

Twenty-eight of us walked over five kilometres to reach the exam venue. We camped there in the nearby primary school for about a week; Akshaya sir was our able custodian. These were the first important exams I had faced, and I went in with the mindset that 'while no amount of preparation is ever enough, I have given my best'.

I also stood by my resolution: once I wrote a paper, I left it behind without overanalysing. To the best of my knowledge, I had answered all the questions of both maths papers accurately, and was quite happy with my performance in science. There was no risk of not passing in Sanskrit, Odia and social studies. And I felt

I had fared reasonably in both the English papers. I had no reason to feel unhappy.

Saying goodbye to the Kasarda High School compound after the exam was a difficult moment, because it also meant saying farewell to all my batchmates. The reality was that I may not be able to meet some of them ever again, but it was not as easy to comprehend at the moment.

Back in Rajuna's quarter, I packed my books and clothes, bid farewell for the time being to him, Mani Bhauja and their four kids, and left for home, carrying the trunk on my head.

After the exams, I got back to a familiar routine, joining Nana and Bhaina in household chores. In the evenings, I sang in the Trinatha Mela, and roamed around with my friends from the village. The Raja Festival was approaching, and I was in the mood to fly kites again, having missed out on the experience the previous year. It was a strange feeling to discover that I had plenty of time at hand; it showed me how much time I had spent studying the whole of the last year.

As I had been away for the most part of the previous years, I had never spoken to Bhaina's wife more than just addressing her as 'Nuabou' and responding to questions with an occasional nod, when necessary. But now, it was time to gel with her. She had taken the initiative with her blessings before the exams, but I felt shy, not knowing how to talk to someone of her age from the opposite gender, except Sanjunani, and Mani Bhauja, who was a bit older.

Those who fear failing an exam never want the results to be announced; those who have a history of great performance are probably not as bothered. I was somewhere in between, in a state of equanimity—sure of passing, even reasonably sure of securing a first division. But where would I eventually land? Good? Excellent?

The process of announcement of the State Board Exam results was antiquated. On the first day, we would come to know from the school office whether one had passed or failed, and if successful, the passing division. But the marks would only be known a few days later.

There were no surprises. I went to the school and heard that I had passed with a first division. Manoj, Bidyadhar and another friend, Rabi, had also secured first divisions. Bini had passed too, in the second division.

'The results are as expected. Come in two days; by then, we would have received the actual marks,' Rajuna said.

That meant another few days in a state of equanimity, but I was content at having given my best. Now, whatever the result was, it would be what I deserved.

On Saturday, Nana had just returned from Kaliaghai Hata, having procured our weekly rations from the proceeds of selling betel leaves. 'Looks like our Dama has done well in the exam. Everyone was talking in Hata today. They were also talking about some record,' I overheard him saying to Bou.

With a racing heart and legs, I reached school. 'You have broken our school record by a good margin of twenty-nine marks!' exclaimed Rajuna, with appreciation I hadn't heard from him before. 'With these marks you should be able to get admission into Intermediate of Science at Ravenshaw College. It is also the beginning of another journey ... a long ... rather, the real journey.'

I knew what he meant, but at that moment I had tears in my eyes—the tears of happiness that one reads about in books and hears about from people. It was my first experience of those.

I did not know how to express gratitude to anyone openly other than looking at them with a teary smile. That is how I looked at Rajuna.

I felt gratitude for every other teacher in school; more for some, less for other. But after Rajuna, if I had real gratitude towards any other person, it was Paiana. He had inspired me, and now I had broken his record, set the previous year, and was on the cusp of following him to Ravenshaw College with a high first division.

There are turning points in life, as well as transformational epochs. Those four years in high school, the three years in Rajuna's quarters, the two years in the company of Paiana—these turned out to be the transformational epoch of my life. Even the slightest negligence or lack of self-reflection on my part could have derailed my future, be it failing to realize the consequences of not working hard, or not paying heed to the affection, gestures of goodwill and support from Rajuna and Paiana. Life probably would have moved on, but on a different track, at a different pace, towards a whole different destination.

The news of my success spread in our village, but there was no culture of special celebration at home, other than offering a diya at the Grameswara Mahadeva temple. Everyone at home was happy, but a more pressing discussion had begun: how to fund my college education?

4

EXPERIENCING THE MAGNIFICENT RAVENSHAW COLLEGE

THE COLLEGE APPLICATION CALLED FOR two passport size photographs, and the place closest to my village that had a studio was the small town of Niali. You made the commute once to pose for the photographs, and then again after a minimum of three days, to collect them. That was the first time I posed for a solo picture. The cameraman was in a hurry. 'Smile!' he said, alerting me while focusing the camera on my face. I attempted to smile, though my main focus was to keep my eyes open. I did not want to ask for a retake that would have cost me another three rupees. After spending three days in agony, hoping that my eyes had stayed open during the flash, when I finally collected the photographs, there was no smile on my face. Instead, a pair of petrified, wide-open eyes stared out from the photograph. And that did make me smile.

One morning, armed with the photos and attested copies of the provisional school leaving certificate, conduct certificate and the board exam marks sheet, I set out for Ravenshaw College. My plan was to collect the admission form, fill it in, and submit it on the same day before returning; it would save me time and money. The bus to Cuttack took over two hours and after getting down at the OMP Square bus stand, I asked for directions, followed a long red boundary wall, and reached the college gate.

'Why is the gate so high? Would anyone try climbing it?' I wondered, awestruck. The line for the application form wound around the huge administrative building, encircling it a few times. I guessed that it would take at least two hours for me to reach the counter, but there was no option: clutching my documents, I crept forward with the line.

My mind drifted to the chance encounter with the block development officer of Niali, who had attested my documents. He had set evenings aside at his residence for attestation, and I submitted three copies of the documents for verification, which were checked and slipped to the bottom of the pile. I was last in line, and after the BDO signed them, the door closed, but I still stood on the verandah, listening to a song playing within his residence. Someone opened the door—it was the BDO himself.

'Do you have your documents for attestation too?'

'No, Sir, I just got them attested by you. But if you kindly permit, I would like to listen to this one song that is currently playing, and then leave.'

'Come inside, then. You don't have to stand outside!' the BDO said, his tone very reassuring.

I entered with a grateful smile. As soon as the song ended, he asked, 'Do you want me to rewind and replay the song?'

Turns out, the song was being played on a cassette, not on a radio as I had thought. I had never seen a cassette player before, so I asked, 'Is that possible, Sir?'

'Yes, I will just do it for you. That way I will also listen to the song. Rarely do I find someone listening to a song so mindfully,' said the BDO, pointing me to a chair.

Once the song had played again, he asked me if I sang, and I responded in the affirmative.

'Why don't you sing now?'

'May I sing the same song that was on the cassette player?'

'That would be just wonderful!'

I sang the title song from the Odia movie *A Nuhen Kahani*, originally sung by my idol Pranab Kishore Patnaik, then ate a couple of biscuits offered by the family's caretaker, drank a glass of water, and was about to leave.

'Show me your marksheet,' the BDO said, and I handed it to him.

'This is fantastic, my boy! You will secure admission wherever you apply! What do you want to be in life?'

'How do I know, Sir? I will just take one step at a time. I am seeking admission into the Intermediate of Science programme for now.'

'You're probably right; you have a long journey ahead. But your career options will unfold before you at the right time. God bless you.'

I expressed my gratitude with a namaskar and left, feeling inspired by his encouraging behaviour, which left a lasting impression on my mind.

'Hello! Move! Can't you see the line has moved quite a bit ahead of you?' The irritated voice of a fellow applicant snapped my mind back to the present—the line for admission into Ravenshaw College. I hurriedly took a few steps forward, then looked down to check if my chappals were still on my feet, still getting used to footwear. Somehow, I thought if I were not mindful, they would just slip away from under my feet.

Around noon, I collected the application form, sat on the veranda and filled in the details, attached the documents, and joined another line to submit the form. I checked everything, submitted it, exited the gate and followed the boundary wall, walking towards the bus stand.

Everything I had seen on campus was painted red: the buildings, the post office and even the boundary wall. I chuckled, recalling the red shirt that had made me the laughing stock on the first day at Bilasuni High School.

The anticipation of studying at Ravenshaw College was exciting. Rajuna felt confident that I would secure admission to this prestigious institution, but also advised me to hedge my bets and apply to at least one other college. That meant more money on applications, but I managed to convince Nana and Bhaina to part with an additional ten rupees for one more application—SVM College, Jagatsinghpur, was chosen as the safe bet.

Jagatsinghpur is hardly twenty kilometres from my village, but going there was tricky. One had to cross three rivers, and there were no bridges, so no direct buses. One had to take a detour to change buses, making it a hundred-kilometre journey one way. That would cost at least fifteen rupees, so the viable option was to commute by bicycle. I set out for Jagatsinghpur with just thirteen rupees in my pocket: ten for the application, twenty-five paisa for postage stamps to be affixed on the self-addressed envelope, one rupee to eat something on my way back, and one rupee seventy-five paisa contingency fund. Things went reasonably well, except for one thing that I had grossly overlooked: the boatman's fee of fifty paisa for each time I had to cross a river—twenty-five for the bicycle and twenty-five for me. So, when I reached Jagatsinghpur, out of the Rs 2.75 budgeted for food and contingency, Rs 1.50 had already evaporated, and I was twenty-five paisa short on boatmen's fees for the return journey, even if I ate nothing.

I said to myself I would figure something out for crossing the last river, but it would be impossible to pedal twenty kilometres on an empty stomach under the scorching sun, so I decided to enter a roadside eatery with just a twenty-five paisa coin in hand. All that I could afford were four slices of bread; I enjoyed pushing every bite down my throat with the help of a glass of water. At least now I had some much-needed energy to pedal back home.

While crossing the last river, I waded through chest-deep water, holding the bicycle high above my head. Far from bothering me, it put a smile on my face, thinking this was just the beginning; the next few years would bring many such challenges. But I was determined to face them with courage.

I did not have to worry about travelling to Jagatsinghpur again, at least for my college education, because soon, the admission letter from Ravenshaw College arrived on time, along with the confirmation of a hostel seat. I would be in the New Hostel, where Paiana was also staying. My eyes lit up thinking about being near Paiana again. 'This is the first fruit of my hard work. Things would not have been as smooth had I not pushed myself as hard in the eleventh standard,' I thought, chuckling happily to myself.

Another piece of good news was that, based on my board marks, I would almost certainly receive the National Talent Search Examination (NTSE) Scholarship, which in those days was a good seventy rupees per month, and a complete refund of the admission fee, irrespective of the college. The only caveat was that it had to be a government college, but that was not a constraint as such, because those were the best in Odisha anyway.

But for me, there was a drawback: the scholarship and the refund of the admission fee were to come later against actuals, after the approval of the government. First, I had to pay a hundred rupees out of my pocket to secure admission—the largest one-time payment I had made for any academic requirement thus far. I was afraid of handling that much cash all by myself, so Bhaina accompanied me to Cuttack this time.

After paying the fees and collecting the receipt, Bhaina and I took a walk on the glorious campus of Ravenshaw College. The front block was the majestic administrative-cum-arts building with a red facade. The science block was another imposing building that ran parallel to the front block. The East and West hostels were on either side of the two main blocks. Looking at the architecture, one could tell that both those hostels must have been constructed along with the main blocks a hundred years ago. All other buildings were later additions, with a different look and feel. We also took a walk to my soon-to-be new home, the New Hostel, about ten minutes' walk from the main blocks. We could not meet Paiana, as the hostels were closed for the summer vacation. Before leaving campus, we made sure to enquire about the opening day of the college as well.

When the time came to depart from my village once more, my sole companion, again, was the trunk that had accompanied me to high school. Only this time, it was almost empty. There were no books; just my clothes and old notebooks with a few empty pages, for use until new notebooks were procured. Kaka, Maa and Khudi had come home to see me off. I bent to lift the trunk on to my head when Bhaina said, 'Let me carry it on the bicycle and walk you to the bus stand'. Nana and Kaka also walked with us. Bou, Nuabou, Maa, Khudi, and Rita had tears in their eyes; I was going farther away from them than I had ever been. Shyama and Mitu were too young to express their feelings.

This was one of many isolated instances early on that appeared insignificant, but had a profound impact on me: seeing my family standing together to wish me well on my journey ahead awakened in me a deep desire to build, strengthen and preserve the sanctity of an inseparable joint family.

The first session I attended at Ravenshaw College happened to be a chemistry class. A humid summer day in coastal Odisha can be challenging, and the discomfort was compounded by a power cut that afternoon. When the power returned, my eyes were riveted to the ceiling fan. The professor hurled a piece of chalk at my forehead to bring my attention back to chemistry. 'Hello, you—the boy in the pink shirt—have you never seen a ceiling fan before?' he thundered. I was shaken up, but still replied with absolute innocence that I had indeed never seen it before.

The entire class laughed, and the interrogation continued with all eyes on me.

'Okay, now tell me, why were you staring at the fan with your mouth wide open?'

'Sir, I was curious to see after how many revolutions I could no longer count the fan blades,' I answered, embarrassed. The class burst into laughter yet again, but by this time, the professor, probably realizing that I was feeling humiliated, ended the episode with a light-hearted comment: 'This is a chemistry class, you are supposed to count atoms and molecules, not fan blades!'

That evening, I had to work with the hostel office on my room allocation. Paiana's room was full, but he had secured a room for me on the same floor. I had dropped off my trunk in his room before going to class; now, I collected the trunk and moved into my room. There were four seats in a square room, one in each corner. Two of them were called 'window' seats, where one could at least open the window and gaze outside, and typically, they were occupied by the second- or fourth-year students. The other two were called 'door' seats, as the beds were on either side of the door.

Sleeping through the first night in the hostel was an experience in itself. I still wonder why almost no one used to be in casual shorts then. The rich folks were in trousers; I was wearing a lungi, the most comfortable attire I could ever imagine. When I had left, Nuabou had slid a bedsheet and a thin pillow into the trunk, and I used both. Falling asleep was never a problem for me, and I had run around so much during the day that I was eager to crash. My eyes fell on the ceiling fan hanging from the centre of the roof, reminding me of my embarrassment in chemistry class, and that made me chuckle as I fell asleep.

Electricity by far was the most intriguing thing during my transition to the college campus. I was curious and even enjoyed fiddling with the toggle light switch. In my room, the switch cover was broken, exposing its innards. I had read in textbooks that touching electric wires and exposed parts would give a shock, but I was curious to experience it. I touched one of the exposed screws, and, oh boy, my roommates were woken up by a loud 'ouch'. I managed a save with an 'I'm sorry' look, but indignantly filled in a page of the hostel's complaint book on my way to class. The switch cover was repaired by the time I returned in the evening.

There were many other 'first time' experiences during those first few days at college. Taking a bath in a bathroom turned out to be more to do with singing than I imagined—even those with tuneless voices turned into singers as soon as the door closed. The area was so noisy that I could barely hear my own voice, so I sang louder. On the one hand, I missed the thrilling experience of swimming in the Board Pokhari or the Hensanaga Pond, but on the other, the freedom of singing at the top of one's voice felt quite liberating. More so, because of the uninterrupted musical accompaniment of the water gushing out of the tap and splattering into the empty plastic bucket below. First it was high pitched and had a heavy rhythm; then, as the bucket began to fill up, the water splashed around more gently, lowering the decibel level. Fortunately, there was no shortage of water. The city of Cuttack itself is on an island between the Mahanadi river and its tributary Kathajodi.

Only lunch and supper were served in the hostel mess, but I had no time to think about breakfast or afternoon tiffin. There was just too much happening. Life was too exciting; I wasn't used to this much freedom.

Managing my own finances was challenging, but empowering too. Classes ran full steam, and the curriculum was mind-boggling; I needed my books and a good night's sleep. In the first month, therefore, after paying the hostel fees in advance, I prioritized buying a mosquito net and books over a new set of clothes.

The biggest problem was that the medium of instruction was no longer Odia, it was English. I struggled to cope, but going back to the habits Rajuna had instilled in me helped. My routine was rigid and rigorous: I woke up early, completing morning rituals before the toilets and bathrooms got crowded, glanced through the chapters that were supposed to be covered during the day, grabbed an early lunch, took the ten-minute walk to the main campus, returned to the hostel, revised the chapters covered during the day, had an early dinner, and finally tried to read for at least another hour before going to bed.

Life became pretty much monotonous, confined to shuttling between the hostel and the main campus. Occasionally, when I absolutely needed it, I stopped by to consult Paiana or went to the famous college square to buy essentials or books.

I craved friends; I wanted to go out with them and explore the city, watch films...I had the freedom, but not the money, and in hindsight, that was a good thing. I single-mindedly focused on studies, determined not to let the syllabus overwhelm me. Like in high school, I began noticing patterns and started handling each subject uniquely: mugging up, memorizing, solving problems, practicing. I did what was needed to handle physics, chemistry, algebra, trigonometry, botany and zoology. I devoted all my time to studies, except on Sunday mornings, when I washed and dried my only set of clothes. Gradually, the subjects seemed under control, except one: Set Theory in mathematics. I still had not thought about English and Odia; they were low on the priority list.

I had discovered one other first year student like me, Basudev Panda (Basu). He was Paiana's roommate. Like me, he had also been wearing the same pants and shirt every single day. Soon, we became friends. Now, I had one more reason to drop in at Paiana's room.

One month of college flew by, and I survived without borrowing any money from anybody. I even managed to save two rupees, just enough to pay the bus fare for the monthly visit home, by surviving on two meals a day. I was among the first to enter when the mess door opened, and while most residents complained about the quality and taste of food, I found it delicious. For them, what mattered was the taste; for me, it was satisfying my hunger.

But skipping breakfast was not a good idea in the long run, as I wasn't very effective on an empty stomach in the crucial morning hours. Basu was smart; he had carried a bag of chivda (flattened rice) from home.

I also realized the need for one more essential item, a wristwatch, as I had already received a few reprimands for arriving late to a few lab sessions.

From the hostel, I had written my first ever letter home, addressed to Bhaina. The return letter was in Nuabou's hand, indicating that the responsibility of communication with me had been delegated to her. I had no complaints; Nana and Bhaina were not as easy to communicate with anyway!

In the letter, I had urged Bhaina to arrange an annual income certificate from the office of the tehsildar, which was mandatory to complete my application for the NTSE scholarship. I had also written about my breakfast woes and the wristwatch.

On my first journey home, I was busy reliving the moments of the past month at college. I soon arrived at Apuja bus stop, from where I boarded the bus to Cuttack, and reached home after a short walk. Bhaina had just returned from his morning errands, and Nana had come back from Kaliaghai Hata. It was Saturday, the day for selling betel leaves in the Hata and buying the weekly rations.

'Would you need additional money this month to buy spare clothes?' Bhaina asked as soon as he saw me.

I was hoping either Bhaina or Nana would initiate this topic, but I had not expected it to come up this soon.

'Is this the time to ask this question? He hasn't even washed his face!' snapped Nuabou.

Fortunately, the question had come from Bhaina; had it been from Nana, Nuabou could not have opened her mouth.

But I went ahead and responded to Bhaina. 'Yes, if possible.'

Bhaina was clearly bothered. 'You need to be mindful while spending.'

I opened the bag and displayed all the new books I had purchased, and explained to Bhaina why buying books was more urgent than spare clothes. I also explained how I had made do with measly expenses, adding how I had not gone out of the campus more than twice, only to buy books and bare essentials. There was no exaggeration, it was all fact. I also told him about staying hungry in the morning, as well as wearing the same clothes every day.

'What do you not believe from what he has been saying? He prioritized books over clothes. But how long could he manage with just one set of clothes? Can you imagine what would have happened if he had washed his clothes and for some reason they didn't dry in time? You want him to bunk classes and sit in his hostel room?' Nuabou argued in support of my plea, as everyone looked at her.

'You need to realize there is no money plant at home,' snapped Bou, looking from Nuabou to me and back.

'Didn't you realize from his letter? He had given a detailed account of his spending. We at least eat pakhala at home; ever thought how he would be studying in the morning on an empty stomach for the entire month?' Nuabou responded.

Everyone at home knew that Nuabou had a soft corner for me, but this time it was not just an expression of empathy; she had presented my situation with pure rationale, better than I could.

I knew there was no money plant at home, though I wished there was! Emotions were riding high, but I needed to remain calm in the moment.

I walked to our backyard and looked up at the sky, then walked through the stretch of bamboo groves and paddy fields till I reached the lone palm tree that stood on the bank of the Marichia Nali. This was 'my spot', where I always found solace.

Bou knew that spot; she followed me after I disappeared through the backyard.

'I am your Bou. If you are offended by my words, how can I say anything to you?' she said, with eyes moist.

'It's not that; I just needed few moments alone, Bou. And I know that we do not have a money plant at home. Do you need to remind me that I was not born with a silver spoon in my mouth? Do you think I don't realize how difficult it is for you to fund my studies?'

I knew what would stop her tears; I wrapped my arm around her shoulder as we walked back home.

Bhaina was not less empathetic to my situation, but there was no money at home. It had to be arranged with great difficulty.

By the time we reached home, Nana and Bhaina had headed out to the Hensanaga pond for a bath. Bou behaved casually, but I knew she was deep in thought: she was the one who managed the relationships with our immediate neighbours, and arranged all short-term borrowings.

I tried to lighten the situation by dragging Bou to the kitchen with a promise to tell her what all happened in college over the last month. Nuabou, Rita, Shyama and Mitu followed. I narrated my experiences in college and the hostel: about staring at the ceiling fan, about the electric shock, about how I felt inside the toilet and bathroom, and how much I had been eating in the hostel mess. Everyone cracked up.

By the time Nana and Bhaina returned, lunch was ready.

'Bring the letter, we will go over the items one by one,' said Bhaina.

'I remember everything,' said Nuabou with a chuckle, while serving lunch. 'I have also located the watch, but it has stopped functioning. This is what happens if you do not use it even once in a year!'

Bhaina added: 'But it can be fixed. Take it to a watch mechanic.'

'A bag of chivda has also been kept aside, so, we have checked two boxes already,' quipped Nuabou.

The serious discussion took place in the evening. Nana was silent all along—he was naturally reflective; listened more and spoke less. But whenever he opened his mouth to ask leading questions, everyone shut up and listened.

'You have already spent one month in the hostel. Going by your experience, how much money do you think you would need per month, bare minimum?' asked Nana.

'Hundred rupees,' I said, having done my homework. 'Sixty rupees towards the mess bill, fifteen rupees towards college tuition, and twenty-five rupees towards buying essential things. But for the first few months things could be different. Like last month, I had to buy most of the books that were urgently needed. This month, I have to buy the two remaining books. I would also need to buy cloth to get trousers and a shirt tailored. There could be some other essentials, like lab record books.'

'What is the likelihood of your getting that scholarship you were mentioning?'

'Almost certain.'

'I have collected our annual income certificate from the tehsildar's office. Do not forget to carry it with you. Complete the application process on priority,' Bhaina interjected.

'Until you receive that scholarship, it will be hard, but your college education will be funded, no matter what. You just focus on your studies,' said Nana, with consensus from Bou, Bhaina and Nuabou.

Rita, Shyama and Mitu were not grown up enough to add to the conversation other than looking at our faces, and sometimes, whispering into each other's ears.

Bou had already put aside a hundred rupees towards my monthly hostel expenses. Now, she had to arrange an additional hundred and fifty rupees at least. Short-term borrowing was not a big issue as such, but the exorbitant interest was. Plus, there was limited income to pay back the loans. However, by the time we sat down for our supper, Bou had managed to borrow the additional money from neighbours. So, I had Rs 250, the annual income certificate, the wristwatch (to be serviced), and a bag of chivda—all ready to go.

As I lay in bed, I reflected on how resolutely the entire family had supported me. My eyes were moist with gratitude.

Upon reaching college, I swiftly got to work—I submitted the NTSE scholarship application, bought my long-awaited English and Odia books, gave the watch for repair, and cleared the hostel mess dues.

There was hilarity the next morning when I soaked two fistfuls of chivda in water and then realized I had no sugar. In any case, I pushed it down my throat. After a few days, I walked to the college square in the evening to collect the watch, and bought a hundred grams of sugar.

The next morning, after soaking the chivda, a brilliant idea struck me: I devised a mind game, and didn't add sugar right away. I gulped down a few scoops of chivda, imagining that I had to eat the same old soaked unsweetened stuff, and just when it felt that the tongue needed a bit of pampering for being so cooperative, I added a tiny bit of sugar. In this way, my experiment ended on a sweet note every morning.

I derived much satisfaction from this little mind game, which not only became a conscious exercise of self-control, but also became a tool for self-development—I learnt to be frugal.

Moreover, since I did not have to rush to the mess for an early lunch, the mornings became more productive. My study schedule could be extended, and the wristwatch helped organize and optimize it further.

After receiving my board exam results, I had secretly started dreaming of becoming a doctor. I thought it was the best profession to serve and stay close to people. But the size of the botany and zoology books gave me jitters. I found no smart way to tackle these subjects; my sure-shot learning technique, mugging up, was falling short.

Another incident dampened my dreams further. In the first ever zoology lab, we were supposed to draw a frog and a toad, side by side, on the same page. My track record in drawing was pathetic— even in school, when I had to sketch something like a banana, I had to write 'banana' underneath. For the evaluator, understanding what I had sketched was like cracking a cryptic code; I was that bad. There was no way I could make freehand sketches of a frog and a toad. I, therefore, traced the sketches from the textbook. I failed in this as well. Supposedly the page had moved a bit while tracing and the belly of the frog became bigger than usual. 'Is it a rainy season frog?' asked the professor, mocking. 'Yes,' I responded innocently. 'Shameless! You can't even sketch a frog correctly?' shouted the professor. He then ripped out the page of my lab notebook and shredded it to bits. I was petrified—my dream of becoming a doctor was being torn to pieces in front of my lab mates.

I consoled myself with the thought that maybe becoming a doctor was a bad dream to have.

The first internal exam was fast approaching, and the most affordable currency I had was not money, but time. I had to maximize it.

Since I had come to the college hostel, I had effectively put to use those valuable five minutes in the bathroom. Five minutes, just enough to sing one complete song, without referring to a piece of paper, with no one watching or judging. It was a creative way to commit time to a social hobby that would win me friends, and most importantly, give me happiness.

Now, those five minutes turned productive too—I found the inside of the toilet quite an effective place to quietly recall the chemistry equations. If I was unable to recollect one, I checked the chemistry book as soon as I returned to my room. If any of my roommates had noticed, they would have wondered what the correlation was between the toilet and the chemistry book!

I also found that the ten-minute walk with Basu to the main campus was the best time to recall and debate assumptions and formulae from physics and mathematics. Basu was a genius; each time we revised something together, I realized how much I did not know.

I was hard on myself; if I ever went to bed early, I'd immediately start practicing something that I had just mugged up, even if it was just for a few minutes. I realized that rote learning became more effective when paired with recall and practice.

The results of the first internal exam boosted my morale. They weren't extraordinary, but nothing concerning either. My sole aim was to ensure I did not get overwhelmed by the unforgiving syllabus, and the English medium of teaching. I had accomplished both, and overcome my fear.

Those were no small achievements at that point in time. I had the will, and I made sure that it rolled on a pair of wheels: hard work and discipline. Undeterred and resolute on the path as a quintessential learner, I had begun to feel less insecure about my career journey.

More than three weeks had elapsed since I left home with Rs 250 in my pocket. I had not gone out of the campus much, and Rs 150 was still left. I went out with Paiana to buy material for a shirt and pants, which cost ninety-five rupees. But I got the shock of my life when I discovered the tailoring cost in Cuttack—a few tailors quoted fifty rupees! The cheapest quote was forty rupees. Just three months ago, in Bilasuni, I had got my first set of pants and a shirt stitched for just twenty-five rupees. I thought why not wait a week or two and get the same tailor to stitch the new clothes when I visit home? The money saved could be put to other use. There was a thrill in living on a shoestring budget, squeezing the maximum value out of every rupee.

One Saturday morning, I was in the lab when I looked at the watch out of habit. Since I started wearing the watch, I just loved flicking my wrist to look at the time every now and then. But that day, my heart skipped a beat. The watch had stopped. Disappointed, I walked out of campus after the lab, and went to the same man who had repaired it. 'The spring needs lubrication and cleaning, and will cost just five rupees. Come at this time tomorrow to collect it,' he said. I had no other option; over the next twenty-four hours, I missed it so much, because it had become such a close companion. The next day, having collected it, I could not refrain from checking it every five minutes. But it only worked for a few days and then, to my dismay, it stopped again. The repairman said he had changed the spring again, and it was back to life, but he added, 'I have tried everything, but the watch is quite old'. The message, clearly, was that if the watch stopped again, he could do no more.

And stop it did. I had spent time and money fixing the watch, prioritizing this over other essentials—spending twenty-five rupees, in vain as it turned out. Twenty-five rupees was a big sum for me. But it was time to let go of the disappointment and move on.

This time when I got home, there was less debate about money. From my letters, everyone knew how hard I had been trying to manage it. They also knew that the watch had been giving me enough trouble, though I didn't tell anyone how much I had spent repairing it.

For me, a watch was not a fashion accessory but an essential item. I approached Kaka, whose watch was never used, but was working. 'I do not need a watch to go to the paddy field or betel farm; take it and put it to use,' he said wholeheartedly.

That was how Kaka was to me—he may have split his household from Nana's, but the emotional bond, especially with me, remained strong as ever. I used his radio the most. Now, it was the turn of the watch.

Nuabou had kept aside another bag of chivda, and this time, a small packet of sugar too.

In hindsight, deciding to get clothes stitched in Bilasuni was a good idea—apart from saving at least fifteen rupees, I also got the chance to see Rajuna, and share the experience from my first two months in college. He felt happy about my marks in the first internal exam. I slept over in his quarters, and got a chance to catch up with Mani Bhauja too.

This was the time when bell bottom pants were the fashion in India. I did not have the freedom to decide the style of my first pair of pants—Rajuna had taken charge and asked the tailor to stitch conservative, straight-cut pants. But this time around, I bought a generous cut of cloth and made my first fashion statement with bell bottoms measuring thirty inches, while my waist measured just twenty-six.

Until then, I had never worn trousers that fit around the waist; they had always been made a few sizes larger so that I could use them longer. Although I shot up in height during my four years at high school, my waist never seemed to expand. Keeping my trousers from slipping right off the waist was a perennial struggle.

Both in high school and college, life followed a similar routine: classes during the day, studies in the mornings and evenings. Even the routine of a monthly visit home continued, though earlier it was to bring homegrown rice as the boarding and lodging fee for Rajuna's quarter; now, it was to bring a bag of homegrown chivda and a hundred rupees that had been secured from the proceeds of selling homegrown paddy or betel leaves.

But there was a big difference between then and now: there was no Rajuna, or any other adult, watching over my shoulder; no guiding hand to keep me on the straight and narrow. I was completely on my own, had the freedom to do whatever I wanted, and also, the ready cash. Though limited, I still had enough to drift into leading an irresponsible life, but I made a conscious decision to impose self-discipline and work towards my goal—to get a good job and lift my family out of scarcity.

I forced myself to live in the company of textbooks. 'How can you not get bored looking at the same set of books, same chapters, same pages over and over again?' mocked a senior roommate once. 'How can you walk to the college square, walk through the same streets, glance at the same shops, and return every evening without having the need to buy anything?'

I could have snapped back, but refrained, later telling him that my whole life lay ahead of me to be able to indulge in materialistic pleasure. But for that, I would need a money plant, and this was the time for me to nurture that money plant.

In Ravenshaw College, most boys came from privileged backgrounds. Tripping up would mean a minor setback for them; they had safety nets. But for me, every time I tripped, I risked sliding right back to where I had come from—a supportive and loving but cash-strapped family. Tripping, therefore, was not in my lexicon; it was not an option.

It is not all that hard to understand what the 'right thing' is, but converting intent into action needs perseverance; converting actions into habits needs consistency. I chose to be my own controller, not of my destiny, but at least of my actions. I was determined to move forward, alone, from the point where Rajuna had let go of my hand.

However, this is not to say that I was a loner. I had a few good friends. I was a nerd, but not a bore. I had Basu to discuss mathematics and physics with, and some others to hang out with. With these friends, I would sing Odia songs, and we'd use the desks and lab record books as drums in some corner of a classroom when, occasionally, any class got cancelled.

A few days before Saraswati puja, the NTSE scholarship was announced. Four hundred and twenty rupees towards the scholarship for the first six months, and an additional hundred rupees towards the full reimbursement of the admission fee: a total of five hundred and twenty rupees.

Within just a few months, I had broken my old record for the largest amount of cash I held in my hands! I wish I had the luxury of doing whatever I wanted with that money. I could have cooked up some story to enjoy at least a part of that money. There was a sense of exhilaration in me, but my conscience nipped it in the bud. Keeping the news a secret for a few days held its own charm though; I wish I had the means to freeze that moment when I handed over the money to Bou, and capture forever the happiness of all the family members at that moment.

A large part of that money was utilized to repay short-term loans. I was given two hundred rupees this time to manage for the next two months. And I did loosen up to some extent as my confidence grew.

I started watching one Odia movie a month. Sometimes, Paiana gave me company, and sometimes it was Basu. A side benefit of this indulgence was that it further whetted my appetite for singing, which was my only source of affordable entertainment. Though I didn't go out of the campus, the loudspeakers from the two adjacent streets of Cuttack, Chhatra Bazar and Malgodam, used to play Odia and Hindi songs nonstop. I was getting good at learning lyrics in a short time, and practice sessions in the bathrooms also served as a nice way to unwind. Singing kept me happy and sane when the pressure and monotony of studying got too much.

After getting my new clothes, for the first time, I decided to strut to class using the route via the ladies' hostel. The path around the western side of the football field was one of two ways to walk from our hostel to the main campus buildings, and no one took that path except Basu and me. Others took the more 'attractive' path, on the eastern side of the field, which put the ladies' hostel on the way.

It wasn't that Basu and I were indifferent to girls; just that we could not walk past the ladies' hostel wearing the same clothes every single day. But at some point, not sure exactly when, my heart longed for Bini's smile.

Bini, her closest friend Jyotshna, and my close friend Bhikari were attending another college. Meeting Bini in person was out of the question, but Bhikari and I were in touch. I got hold of Bini's address from him and, with a trembling heart and hand, wrote her my first letter. When, some time later, I opened her first letter to me, I wish I could have measured my racing pulse.

Soon, a year had flown by since I started at Ravenshaw, and I felt good looking back. I could have done better in the annual exams, but I had tackled all the challenges of my new life with determination, and most importantly, not slipped off my path.

My summer vacation did not go to waste; I used it to get a strong grip on the subjects that had given me trouble, especially the Set Theory in mathematics. By this time, my proficiency in English had also improved.

My studying habits had an influence on my younger siblings, especially Rita. Shyama was not good at studies, but had to sit with us through the evening. That's when I overheard a conversation between Nana, Bou and Nuabou that comforted me.

'The scholarship came to our rescue this year. Dama needed about a hundred rupees a month, out of which seventy rupees got covered through the scholarship. If he continues to concentrate on his studies and keeps receiving scholarships, we should be able to support his studies without much sweat,' Nana said.

Having self-belief is one thing; creating the right impression to gain the trust of family members is another altogether. No one had seen how hard I had been studying in the hostel, nor did they have the ability to understand my progress card to check how I was doing. The only driving factor was love, understanding and trust in the family.

That summer vacation was the last time I flew kites with my buddies from the village—Tipa, Nagana, Kunia and Nirua—and produced a jaw-dropping moment.

A bird just glided on its flight path and sat on the top edge of my kite. Rectangular kites are known for their stability when flying against steady wind, and my kite was rather a big one, but still, it started sinking as soon as the bird landed on it. As it descended a bit, the bird lost balance, flapped its wings and started flying, and instantly, the kite started soaring to its original altitude. The bird was persistent. It completed a looping flight and returned to land on the kite again and again, for a few more times. Since then, I have yearned for a bird to come and sit on my kite, but it has never happened again.

Soon, the vacations were over, and the crucial second year began. I was determined to hit the ground running.

Basu was the most intelligent human being I had come across, by far. I felt like a phony around him. He was the only one in our entire batch to have cracked IIT-JEE in the first year; this was no small feat, as by the end of first year, only half of the IIT-JEE syllabus was covered. He had declined the offer of admission though, as, in his opinion, he did not secure a great rank.

I changed rooms and joined him as roommate in the second year, with his company serving to pump up my ambitions too. We had two other roommates—our batchmate, Bipin Bihari Choudhury, and a first-year student, Rabinarayan Das. We came together on purpose; basically, all four of us were nerds.

In the second year, many of our batchmates enrolled in special coaching for JEE. That not only required additional money, but also demanded more time, which would have to be carved out of preparations for the Intermediate of Science exam. I could not risk it. What if I could not get through the JEE? I needed good results in the Intermediate exam, which could open doors to a few avenues. That much was clear to me.

The JEE coaching focused on solving numerical problems, so I chose to focus on the academic curriculum but with added emphasis on numerical problem-solving. That helped me prepare for JEE and the Intermediate exam simultaneously.

Conversations had already started at home about funding the next phase of my studies. Nana, Bou and Bhaina had done their math—one quintal of paddy was being sold for about a hundred rupees, and the NTSE scholarship for engineering or medical programmes was Rs 170. Their plan was to set aside twenty-four quintals of paddy towards my higher education.

Everything was going according to plan till a disaster struck our village—the 1980 flood. I was on my monthly visit home and got stranded, so I witnessed the devastation first-hand, and was also old enough to comprehend its consequences. As soon as the water started receding along the bus route, Nana, Bhaina, Bou and Nuabou chased me away from home, saying, 'We will see what needs to be done. But how will it help if you stay on here? Return to the hostel and focus on your studies.'

I hit the books as hard as I could—I would describe the next six months, from October 1980 to March 1981, as the most gruelling phase of my student life. The final exams got over in April, and I did well. The date for the IIT-JEE was in May. Though I did not undergo any special coaching, I was confident of securing a reasonable rank. But destiny had other plans: I developed a mysterious abscess in the lower part of my left hip, which made walking difficult. Basu and I hired a cycle rickshaw to travel to the exam centre, where I could not sit, so I wrote the papers standing at an awkward angle, leaning over the desk. I weathered the first day somehow, but the second day was excruciating. The papers, overall, were forgettable.

The Odisha state JEE for admission into the regional engineering colleges (renamed NITs now) and the other state engineering colleges was to follow two weeks later. I was praying and hoping to get well by then.

The state JEE exam turned out to be equally exacting—a hundred multiple-choice questions spread across four sections, to be answered in three hours, with negative marking! I strategized wrong, starting with maths, followed by physics. I was able to answer most of the questions from these two sections, but they were too time-consuming, and I barely had ten minutes left for the last section, chemistry. In those ten minutes, I was still able to answer around ten questions, but I was miserable when the invigilator snatched away my answer sheet.

As Basu and I exited the exam hall, we overheard many aspirants boasting about their performance. Some had apparently answered every single question with time left over to check the answers. That made me more jittery. After messing up the IIT-JEE, I was banking heavily on doing well at least in the state JEE. But I was afraid that I could no longer hope for a rank. I felt nervous about the future, and also infuriated at myself.

But Basu's words helped reduce my anxiety. He too had gone about the papers like me and had left many questions from the last section unanswered. I felt a glimmer of hope.

The hostels closed after the state JEE; it was time to pack my trunk and leave.

This time, the trunk was weighed down with books. I hired a cycle rickshaw to transport it to the OMP bus stand in Cuttack. But once I disembarked at Apuja, I slipped into my old ritual of balancing the trunk on my head till I reached home.

'Why did you carry it yourself? You could have left it at Patro Mausa's shop in Apuja bus stop and I could have picked it up on the bicycle,' Bhaina said kindly, while helping to take the load off my head. I replied with a smile that it was all the same, as everyone at home looked on.

'How were the exams?' asked Bhaina.

'All good, to the best of my knowledge,' I said, not wishing to pass on my anxiety to anyone at home.

For the next few weeks, I felt disoriented and lonely without my constant companions, books.

The result of Intermediate exams was announced in early June. I had never expected such good results—I could now walk into the general science stream of any college of choice in the country, or even into BITS Pilani for an engineering degree. But BITS was far too expensive, and therefore, not for me. My best bet was the government engineering colleges. They were the best in the country, with a minimal fee.

I was still toying with the idea of appearing for the medical JEE that was yet to be held, but I was a bit nervous about it. I was leaning more and more towards continuing at Ravenshaw College, with a major (honours) in geology, with physics and mathematics as minors.

But soon, the decision was made for me, when the Odisha state engineering JEE results were announced in the Odia daily newspaper, *Samaj*.

Apart from my own, I remembered one other roll number—that of Basu—and not surprisingly, he had scored the number one rank.

But to my pleasant surprise, I did not have to scroll too far down the list to spot my roll number. My rank was good enough to secure admission in any of the disciplines in any of the engineering colleges in the state. I got hold of a copy of the newspaper and pedalled back home as fast as I could.

5

METAMORPHOSIS AT REC ROURKELA

I HURRIED INTO THE COURTYARD in my village home, exclaiming, 'Bou, I got through the engineering entrance exam!' Propping the bicycle against the wall and unfolding the newspaper in hand, I continued, 'I will need to travel to Rourkela now for counselling and securing admission.'

Everyone at home felt joyous; Nuabou was most ecstatic, saying, 'After four years, my diara (husband's younger brother in Odia) will become an engineer!'

Since the high school board exams, the mood at home simply mirrored my mood. When I felt happy, no one needed to understand why—they assumed something had gone right with my exams. But when I felt sad, everyone understood that it was something to do with how to finance my studies.

Everyone's peace of mind, thus, rested on me, but that huge responsibility never added extra pressure. In fact, it served as a constant reminder to be more responsible and keep doing well.

Bou was curious about my choice of engineering, enquiring, 'Didn't you always aspire to be a doctor?'

'Yes, I did. Doctors serve people, and that way, they naturally remain close to people. But I can fulfil that aspiration by becoming an engineer too. Well, not quite. But building bridges and roads, constructing beautiful, affordable houses, laying irrigation canals and railroad networks—this could be as noble a service to mankind as treating patients, isn't it?' I said.

Bou knew it was a half-hearted argument that I was pushing wholeheartedly, but nevertheless, she nodded her head in support.

The decision to choose engineering over medicine was based on a larger truth—the medical entrance exam was yet to be held, and its result was to be announced only in October. I did not want to sit at home in a state of ambiguity for another four months. Moreover, the medical curriculum took at least a couple of years longer than engineering, and my family did not have the wherewithal to support a longer educational path. At that juncture, it was the time to take a head-over-heart decision, and it was prudent to pursue something that would land me a decent job as quickly as possible.

As the topic of my travel to Rourkela came up, fortuitously, Bou recalled Goli Mausi (every lady of Bou's age in my village was my 'maternal aunt'!). Her husband, Bijayaram Mohapatra (whom I addressed as Mausa) worked in the Rourkela Steel Plant. 'They could be helpful in a new place,' said Bou, so I collected their address and sent a letter. The response arrived promptly, written by their youngest son Samir, and featured a warm and welcoming tone.

In the meantime, the intimation letter from Regional Engineering College, Rourkela, also arrived, inviting successful candidates to take part in counselling and decide on their respective engineering streams. There were only two engineering colleges in Odisha then: REC Rourkela, which was later renamed the National Institute of Technology (NIT), and the University

College of Engineering (UCE), Burla. Being government colleges, there was no 'capitation fee'; the one-time admission fee was Rs 457, and that included one month of mess bills and some security deposits.

During my two years at Ravenshaw College, I had realized that arranging monthly recurring expenses, though challenging, was still manageable. It was the occasional one-time spikes that made everyone at home gasp.

Impulsively, I set out to meet a few relatives, especially those with good financial standing. Without the knowledge of anyone at home, I was able to raise around Rs 300 from three of the well-wishers I respected most: Pisa (Rajuna's father), Bhikari Mamu (Bou's younger brother) and Rohit Mamu (Bou's adoptive brother).

I did not know how everyone at home would feel, but at some point, I had to reveal the fact that I had solicited some funds.

'Why did you do this? Don't you have confidence in Nana and Bhaina?' Nuabou reacted with a heavy heart.

Bou was also clearly unhappy. 'Learn to count your blessings. Everyone has their own share of worries. Why would we expect anyone to partake in our struggle? If we need to borrow funds for your education, of course we will, and we will repay them when our situation allows. Why should you approach them with a begging bowl?'

'Should I return the money, Bou?' I suggested.

'No, that would make us look arrogant. All three who have contributed towards your admission fee are your well-wishers. Never ever forget their gesture. But remember one thing—grab the earliest opportunity to return the favour when you stand up on your own feet.'

The message from Bou was loud and clear. I realized that asking financial favours from relatives would hurt sentiments at home. I put my arm around Bou's shoulder and held her tight; that was my way of accepting my mistake and seeking her forgiveness. After Bou, I turned towards Nuabou. A rueful smile was all it took to soothe her.

By bus or train, the commute to Rourkela was an overnight affair. At the time, there were no direct trains connecting two of the biggest cities in Odisha, Cuttack and Rourkela. One had to take a circuitous route via Kharagpur in West Bengal, and trains also usually ran late. A twelve-hour night journey by bus, though tedious, was still preferable, as one was at least assured of a seat. Moreover, compared to trains, the fare was five to ten rupees cheaper.

A thirty-six-hour round-trip by bus completed a milestone transition in my career journey: I attended the counselling session at REC Rourkela, finalized my admission in civil engineering, and then stopped by at Mausa and Mausi's residence and got acquainted with them and their three children.

The classes were supposed to commence in three weeks. When the time came, I boarded the bus to Rourkela, with the same old companion—the trunk. On previous occasions, it contained a pair of chappals, but this time, it had a pair of new shoes. These were a must-wear, else one would invite the wrath of senior students' ragging.

This was an unruly practice at REC Rourkela, and to escape the torture, I frequently fled from the hostel to Mausa's house. In the process, accidentally, I discovered another batchmate of mine, Suvash Chandra Naik, whose uncle's house was opposite Mausa's. Suvash was a year senior to me at Ravenshaw College, and out of respect, I addressed him as Suvash bhai. Ragging primarily took place in the evenings and on weekends, and Suvash bhai and I used to flee from college together most days after the classes got over, and returned to the hostel early the next morning.

My batchmates reacted to ragging in different ways: like me, most of them would abscond during the evenings, ending up in public parks or cinema halls. Consequently, I watched two popular Hindi movies of that time, *Love Story* and *Ek Duuje Ke Liye*. There was no ban on smoking in public parks in those days, and I was enticed by friends into having a few cigarettes.

The ragging sometimes went to the extent of physical abuse at the hands of a few cruel seniors; it got excruciating. But not all of it was bad, especially for someone like me, who came from a rural background and was not exposed to the outside world.

I chuckle recalling this hilarious encounter: as a fresher, when you met someone senior, you were supposed to wish him 'good morning sir', and whether the response was warm or cold, you would add 'thank you, sir'. On one occasion, while returning from Mausa's house, I chanced upon a senior, who was going the other way riding a bike. Seeing him slow down, I stopped and wished him, 'Thank you, sir!'

Applying the brakes, he asked, 'Why are you thanking me?'

In utter confusion, I muttered, 'Sorry Sir!'

'Why are you sorry?'

Lowering my gaze, I said, 'Good morning, sir!'

He smiled and offered to drop me to my room on his bicycle.

A chill ran up my spine as he made me sit on the crossbar in front of his seat—typically, this is how seniors whisked away freshers into their rooms and ragged them. But this guy turned out to be different. Seeing me petrified, he said comfortingly, 'You are a bright guy, else you would not be here'. Just before dropping me under the portico of my hostel, he quipped, 'You must work on your spoken English, else you will face more ragging.'

Recovering from the shock, I reflected on his words. He was right: spoken English would hurt me not only during ragging, but also in my professional and personal life. I also knew that things weren't going to change overnight, but I needed a candid reminder from time to time.

It was also during this period of ragging that I came across another senior, who continues to be one of my few idols. My first encounter with him was no less dramatic than a scene from a Bollywood movie.

I was once picked up by a bunch of second year students and was being ragged in a room. This time, fortunately, it was not physical.

'What is your hobby?' quizzed a senior.

'Singing.'

'Sing a song!'

'I sing only serious Odia songs.'

'Sing seriously, then!' he said, and the room exploded with laughter. I felt quite embarrassed.

'Can you sing the song '*Hrudayara Ei Shunyataku*'?' enquired another senior.

'Yes, that is one of my favourite songs.'

'Sing it, then.'

I sang, and as soon as it ended, I heard a knock on the door. One of the seniors opened and held the door, and everyone in the room cheered as another senior entered the room carrying a bag. I only realized later that he was famous in the college because not only did he play the tabla (an India percussion instrument), but was also an accomplished classical singer. He was nicknamed 'Sangeet Samrat' (emperor of music). Calmly, he unzipped the bag, took out his tabla set, and started tuning it. He made me sing one song after another, accompanying me with his mesmerizing tabla beats. Someone was keeping track of how many songs and how long I sang: thirty-five songs over three hours. They were amazed how I remembered the lyrics of so many songs. 'This is the result of my committed practice in the bathroom,' I chuckled to myself. Sangeet Samrat's actual name was Sanjay Das, and I fondly called him Sanjay bhai.

In the first semester, I distinctly remember one of the sessions by our professor, R.V. Burra, who is now deceased. He was teaching us applied mechanics, a paper that historically gave jitters to the students. After seeing the dismal performance by most of the students in the first internal exam, he issued a warning: 'Going by the trend from past years, almost half of the class will fail in this paper!'

The statement gave me a sinking feeling. But Burra continued, 'Those who would fail will make excuses about not being able to cope with the syllabus due to ragging. And it is ironic that mostly these will be the ones indulging in ragging their juniors in the future.'

Burra was by far one among the most admired professors I came across. Taking a cue from his uninspiring yet candid remarks, I stopped panicking about ragging. Instead of fleeing from the hostel, I stayed back in my room and stubbornly immersed myself in books again.

Already a month had passed, and my performance in the first internal exams had been quite average. I began the recovery process by focusing on applied mechanics first, and giving it closer attention, I realized that it was really nothing to be scared about. It was a nice blend of applied physics and applied mathematics, calling for perseverance in numerical problem solving.

But there was one genuine problem—I did not have a scientific calculator. To be fair, a few other batchmates of mine did not have one either, so I learnt to manage using log tables.

I did well in the first semester compared to most of my batchmates, particularly in applied mechanics. At the time of writing this chapter, I checked my marksheets out of curiosity: I had scored only eleven out of twenty in the internal exams, but seventy-four out of eighty in the university exam. Eighty-five out of hundred in this paper was among the highest in our entire batch.

Even after the frequency and fear of ragging reduced, I continued to visit Mausa's family almost every other weekend. Their three children—Babu, Samir and Gita—were extremely bright. Babu was a year younger than me and quite reserved, but Samir was extremely jovial. He was in his final year of high school and sought my help whenever I happened to be around. Gita adopted me as a brother by tying a rakhi on my wrist on the day of Raksha Bandhan, and continued the tradition for all the four years I was at the REC. I found myself added seamlessly into another lovely family, away from my own: first it was Rajuna, and then it was Bijayaram Mausa.

Like Basu in Ravenshaw College, during my four years of engineering, I was positively influenced by several of my batchmates. Suvash bhai was socially quite active, and had a few close relatives in Rourkela. I accompanied him often to their houses, and expanded my social network. One of the families that I remember fondly consisted of Sushama Nani, Nabaghana Bhaina, and their two lovely daughters, Sanju and Suja.

Another batchmate, Siba Charan Pradhan, was a genius and quite a thinker. We were roommates during our first and second years, and technical discussions with him were engaging and enriching. Ashutosh Dash came from a relatively well-to-do family, and was both intelligent and witty. At the drop of a hat, he could crack a joke and lighten up a rather depressing ambience. I loved his company. Chittaranjan Patra was compassionate; I felt comfortable sharing anything and everything with him. Satya Narayan Panda was the topper of our batch, who provoked me to aspire for more; I loved giving him a run for his money.

But Amulya Prasad Panda, as a friend, was unique. Coming from a similar background to mine, he was fun-loving and genuinely enjoyed my company because of my impromptu singing habit. But those were not the reasons for which I still remember him. During my second semester, I had a mysterious lung infection, and the college dispensary was not equipped to treat anything more complicated than the common cough and cold. Through Bijayaram Mausa, I had somehow arranged an outpatient card to visit Ispat General Hospital (IGH), and though consultation and medicines were for free, the five-kilometre commute to the hospital was a herculean task. I was feeling so weak during those months that I was unable to ride a bike.

The hospital was located in hilly terrain, and on most summer afternoons, the temperature in Rourkela touched 45 degrees Celsius. Moreover, everyone scrambled for time to deal with the demanding syllabus. And yet, Amulya gave me a ride to the IGH, not once or twice, but at least a dozen times.

The treatment as an outpatient did not go anywhere, so the doctor recommended hospitalization. The 'arranged' outpatient card was not a legitimate one, and getting hospitalized using it was risky, so my treatment had to be abandoned. I did not have money to get treated elsewhere. In our family in those days, we were used to tolerating illness and getting used to the pain. If the illness lasted longer or the pain became unendurable, we visited a government dispensary.

Luckily for me, that situation did not arise. I cannot recall how I got cured eventually, nor how long it took. The best answer I could give was that I had recovered 'somehow'. But one thing I do recall is that I was moved by Amulya's compassion, and in my conscience, I had committed to remaining a lifelong friend to him.

In Ravenshaw College, I had realized and maximized 'time' as a powerful currency. At the REC, I nurtured yet another—'social currency'.

In the Rourkela institution, there was no struggle for food, as the hostel served all four meals, including non-vegetarian fare, three times a week, and a monthly feast where a roasted quarter chicken would be served. It was absolute bliss chewing the chicken bones, inch by inch, to dust. Being in a boys-only hostel, a few like me would walk into the kitchen in a lungi and a vest. Life was unsophisticated. On average, monthly expenses ran to around Rs 300, out of which Rs 170 got covered by the NTSE scholarship, although I wish its disbursement had been regular, so that there wouldn't be unforeseen spikes in the need for money from home. But never mind, two semesters out of eight had passed by, and I was ready to enter the second year. Looking around me, I had done quite well compared to most of my friends. Some of them had big dreams, whereas I just wanted another six semesters to go by somehow, so that I could land a job.

I was among the rare few who wore bell-bottom pants. They were already out of fashion, but I still wore them because they still fitted well around my waist, and the zips worked! After a semester exam got over, the rich guys would go for movies non-stop (as if they never went for movies during the semester), while quite a few students would loiter around the residential and shopping areas. They even knew the localities and houses in which beautiful girls could be spotted. Some, who hailed from nearby towns, would pack their bags for a quick overnight trip home.

I had a good handle over my youthful exuberances. I might have borrowed a cycle and visited Mausa's house one evening, or spent a bit more time singing to some friends outside the bathroom, but as quickly as possible, I would pick up the books and start poring over the subjects that would be taught in the upcoming semesters. Closer to the semester exams, especially the night before a difficult paper, most batchmates would study the entire night, but I could never be productive in that kind of spike in study hours. Handling the agony of financial spikes was enough; I believed in putting in a steady effort throughout the semester. And it worked for me.

Frequent reviews of the study material also helped knowledge retention. While many of my batchmates were skipping baths in the morning and showing up in the exam hall with bloodshot eyes, I enjoyed my daily quota of sleep, bathroom singing and breakfast, and walked to the exam calmly recalling important points, and sometimes, even humming.

In many ways, I was an odd duck. That does not mean awkward; it was not a bad thing. It played to my advantage, because I could stay focused on activities and habits that truly mattered, and remained oblivious to distractions.

During the summer vacation that year, I coached my younger siblings in their studies. As I was spending more time at home, Nuabou took notice of one thing. 'You have not been drinking an adequate amount of water. That is the main reason for your illness,' she said, forcing me to drink more. I smiled, with an 'am I a kid or what?' gaze, but she gave me an earful, and then handed me a glass from her limited reserve and ensured it travelled with me to the hostel.

One piece of news that summer that made everyone in the family rejoice was that Nuabou had finally conceived, six years after her marriage to Bhaina. But no matter how simple and under-control you try to keep everything, life continues to test you and complicate matters.

A month into third semester came the heart-wrenching news that she had given birth to a stillborn male baby. Our family was used to enduring financial hardships, but our hearts were not resistant to misfortunes. I sobbed as I held the letter, and my roommate Manoranjan took it and read it.

Bhaina had aptly described the feeling of woe at home. But Manoranjan read out a beautiful bit to try and console me. 'Nuabou, upon recovering from trauma, said that my elder son, Dama, is studying engineering in Rourkela, so why should I cry about a stillborn baby? I am not going to cry anymore ... Nuabou has been consoling herself by picturing you as her elder son. You, therefore, do not cry. Just focus on your studies,' Bhaina had written.

Some relationships are hardcoded by birth, and some get softcoded through behaviour. Nuabou, since then, became my nua Bou (new mother).

Our village had still not recovered from the devastating aftermath of the 1980 flood, when another massive flood hit the Mahanadi Delta in 1982. I was in my third semester. Reading the newspaper about the havoc caused by the flood in our area was painful. I was about to write home for money, but how could I? Impulsively, I decided to bunk classes for about a week and set out to visit my village. I had fifty rupees with me, barely enough for the bus fare one way. But I thought of preserving that money, opting to travel by train for the first time ever, because that way I could travel without ticket (WT, as it is commonly known). Due to the flood, the trains to Cuttack were running almost empty, so it was easy to move from one compartment to another to dodge the travelling ticket examiner. But I couldn't dodge the authorities at Cuttack station, and when I was stopped by a TTE at the exit gate, I earnestly confessed that I had travelled from Rourkela without a ticket. I showed him my college identity card, and told him about the grim floods in my village. Out of sympathy, he let me exit the station.

Reaching home from Cuttack was not easy; buses did not ply beyond a point. After walking the last stretch of ten kilometres, sometimes in knee-deep water on the road, I reached home. Agony and helplessness had gripped the entire village. 'People are fleeing to places of safety. You are forcing yourself into this grim situation' was the chorus that greeted me. Everyone at home disapproved of my impromptu arrival, and nagged me to return to the hostel, repeating, like a broken record, 'we will deal with the situation at home; you focus on your studies'.

After a couple of days, I left with whatever money there was at home.

I knew what the situation at home would be like that for the entire year following the flood. I had already overheard the discussion: Bhaina and Nuabou would stubbornly try not to borrow money; whatever paddy was set aside to be sold to fund my education would not be repurposed; the emphasis would be shifted to rabi crops to offset the loss of kharif crops, and one more betel leaf farm would be planted as soon as the flood receded.

I knew the meals at home over the upcoming year would look quite different: a normal meal at home was 'rice and dal', meaning rice as entrée to fill the stomach, and a tiny portion of dal as a side dish to add flavour. After the destruction caused by the flood to the paddy crop, the meal at home would change to 'dal and rice'. But the dal used as entrée would not be the normal toor dal, or moong dal, or masoor dal; it would be kulthi bean (horse gram). Kulthi bean, in powder form, could yield more quantities of dal of reasonable consistency to fill the stomach. Meant to be used as fodder and occasionally by humans, it would become the main food at home. It would taste okay for the first few days, but soon, it would feel like punishment.

How could I eat a good meal in the hostel mess when everyone at home was forced to eat kulthi bean? Our contrasting situations frequently brought tears to my eyes.

I contemplated offering tuitions to high school and Intermediate Science students. I would not have been the only one; a few of my batchmates were already resorting to that to fund their education, but it was affecting their studies. To my benefit, almost half of the funding requirement for my education was covered by the NTSE scholarship. Bou and Nuabou's reaction to raising money from close relatives at the time of my admission into the REC was also playing in my mind. I decided against it.

In hindsight, the sacrifice and the unwavering support of my family fuelled my resolve to make a great career.

I did not travel home during the short Christmas holidays that year, as the bus fare would have far exceeded the cost of living. I managed my meals economically, visited Mausa's house a bit more often, and remained singularly focused on studies.

The Raja Festival was a subdued affair that year, not just at our home, but for every family on whom the flood had left its unforgiving imprint. Short-term borrowing from neighbours was a daunting task. The thought of short-term borrowing by pawning Nuabou's necklace surfaced, but the pawn brokers were demanding exorbitant interest rates. Bhaina and Nuabou were antagonistic to the idea of borrowing money at such a high interest rate, especially knowing very well that we could never repay the loan anytime soon.

Despite our acute financial problems, we had never thought of selling a part of our agricultural land, but now, there seemed no other option. Nuabou had noticed Bhaina's moist eyes when this was being contemplated. 'What is the use of this necklace? It is losing its lustre around my neck. Just take it and sell it! I will not wear a necklace until Dama buys me a bigger and better necklace with his own salary,' Nuabou had said, pleading with Bhaina. That was her only necklace, our family's gift to her at the wedding. Bou wept upon hearing Nuabou, but that is what had to happen: Nuabou's necklace was sold to fund my engineering education.

From the third year of college, the hostel accommodation rules allowed for each student to get his own room. The rooms on the first floor were in great demand, then came the ones on the top floor which, though comparatively hot, were at least airy. I intentionally picked a room that no one would ever want—the last room of the first block on the ground floor. That was the quietest room in the hostel; I was getting used to so much privacy. I found it most suitable for indulging in many activities that are best done in private, including studying. For the first time, I had a full room to myself, to sing whatever I wanted to sing; I did not have to wait my turn outside a bathroom. Suvash bhai took up the adjacent room, and we loved to lean on each other's shoulders during difficult times. Together, we derived small pleasures from life, including the occasional shared cigarette, and walking the shortest route to the 'back post' for a tea break.

That year, during summer vacations, I had overheard conversations at home regarding my marriage. I was barely halfway through the engineering curriculum, and there was talk about quite a few alliances already. I was an eligible bachelor in the eyes of many of our distant relatives, and some of them even tried to lure Bou and Nuabou by pledging they would take complete responsibility of funding the remaining years of my education. But I was adamant that this was not the time to think about marriage, and I told Bou and Nuabou not to waste any time on it before leaving for college.

My feelings for Bini were a well-kept secret, and though time was not ripe, I thought I must express my feelings before it got too late. The conversations regarding my marriage provided the impetus, and I thought, 'who knows, there might be similar conversations happening in Bini's house on the topic of her marriage'. I wrote her a letter.

A few weeks passed, and the yearning for a response soon turned into anxiety. I could not even be sure that she had received my letter.

Bini was pursuing her MA in Sanskrit at Utkal University in Vanivihar, Bhubaneswar. I thought to myself that I have just been a friend to her all along, and instead of nagging her with letters, I could wait and ask her face to face, on the way home during the Christmas holidays. With that, I forced myself to stay focused on the fifth semester curriculum.

After waiting for a couple of months, I reached her hostel, but she was not there. I felt disheartened, as I had already let her know I was coming to see her. So, I set out to meet her in her department. Standing at the entrance of the lecture hall, I pleaded to the professor: 'I want to talk to Sairindhree (Bini's first name) Mohapatra. It is urgent.' The professor called out her name, and she looked embarrassed.

Though we had been in touch through letters, I had not seen her for quite a long time. She was still the same: always smiling.

We stood in the corridor for a minute, and she didn't look at my face. I had to break the silence.

'I had written a letter to you. Did you receive it?'

'Yes.'

'You did not reply?'

'I will reply.'

The smile on her face was subtle, and that felt comforting. But one couldn't draw a conclusion because she would smile for no apparent reason, even when she felt embarrassed, which was the very reason I had fallen for her. I did not insist on an answer right there, maybe because I did not have the nerve to hear a 'no'.

She still stood with her head down.

'I will wait for your reply,' I said.

She didn't respond.

'Should I leave, then?'

Still no response.

What could her silence mean, I wondered. Yes? No? Worse— was she in love with someone else? Should I invite her for a cup of tea to the cafeteria? I contemplated that for a moment, but I had just pulled her out of the class, and she might not appreciate the gesture, so I dropped the idea.

'Maybe you did not like the way I went about it, but what I wrote to you in that letter was what I was waiting to tell you all these years. I wish we could have conversed a bit today, but you will not speak even a word. You might be eager to return to the class, so I am leaving for now. I will wait for your reply,' I said and left.

I wished she would call out my name, and I would turn back with hope and anticipation. Alas, that was not to be. I did turn back after taking a few steps, but she was gone.

Did I just commit the biggest blunder of my life, I wondered. No; had I not expressed my feelings, I wouldn't have forgiven myself for the rest of my life. I may not like the outcome, but I did like my action.

After the Christmas holidays, I was back at the college hostel, when I received a letter. Familiar inland letter, familiar handwriting, just a small paragraph. But it was not just a simple 'no'; the tone of the letter was quite hurtful. My racing heartbeat slowed down dramatically, much quicker than it had risen.

It was not that I never had a crush on anyone else, but whenever I developed such a feeling, Bini's smiling face would flash before my eyes.

I felt devastated, but did not have a reason to be mad at her. It was just a one-sided feeling after all, I said wistfully to myself. The more I tried to recuperate, the more it began to hurt; the only recourse was to immerse myself in studies.

In the fifth semester, we had a paper on environmental engineering. No one ever scored very high marks in this theoretical paper. Out of eight questions, one had to attempt any five. To my amusement, there were three numerical problems that year, very different from the sample problems given in the reference books. Most of my batchmates, therefore, chose to answer the remaining five theoretical questions. A few of them attempted one numerical problem at the most, but I braved all three. It was a habit to match answers with each other after exiting the exam hall, and after realizing that almost no one had attempted those numerical questions, I began to feel nervous. What if I got them all wrong? A sense of uncertainty crept in. 'Why did you take such a risk?' The more my friends asked this question, the more I felt the ground disappear beneath my feet.

But wait, what if I got all the three numerical questions right? That glimmer of hope soothed me; after all, I had answered two theory questions very well, so there was no way I was going to fail. I felt better and focused on the remaining papers.

Sandwiched between a short winter and a lengthy summer, spring in Rourkela felt especially pleasant. There was a buzz on campus: that year marked the beginning of a festive tradition of

REC Rourkela hosting the annual inter-college spring festival in eastern India. My ritual of five minutes of dedicated practice in bathrooms, the habit of impromptu singing at the behest of friends, and rendering Pranab Kishore Patnaik's soul-searching songs with as much devotion as possible paid dividends: I was selected to represent our college in the vocal music category.

The spring of 1984 has remained vivid in my memory, and the festival wasn't the only reason. Soon after its conclusion, I received another letter from Bini; this time, she had consented to us getting married!

Till then, I had blamed myself for proposing to Bini prematurely and hurting whatever feelings we had for each other. But after reading this fresh letter, I felt relieved. While I was processing my feelings, I received yet another letter from her, and in this one, she was desperate to hear from me.

I felt elated, but wondered why she had been so rude in her reaction to my proposal in the first place. Was she making a compromise now? I wanted to understand.

At the time, forty years in the past, society was dramatically different. Bini and I were from different castes, and we would have to first overcome stiff resistance from home and relatives. But I vowed to set a precedent in my village with an inter-caste marriage.

That was not the only challenge; the concept of 'love marriage' itself was sort of a taboo in the hinterlands of Odisha. But to my advantage, I enjoyed the unconditional love and affection of Bou and Nuabou, and both were vulnerable to emotional blackmail from me. Nana would be a tough nut to crack, but I had Rajuna on my side, who could influence him. Overall, I sketched a robust strategy in my mind to turn our love marriage into an 'arranged' one.

I wrote back to Bini, requesting patience. 'I am overjoyed to read your response, and am still soaking it in. However, I have a few things to say. They are simple, but important to discuss before we agree to walk together. Could we wait until I come and see you during summer vacations?' I wrote.

Meanwhile, the results of the fifth semester were announced, and I was in for a surprise—I had scored the highest marks in environmental engineering! We had one other paper that semester, irrigation engineering, and though it was also a theoretical paper, I somehow found it refreshing and engaging—maybe because I felt it connected to my roots. Overall, for the first time, I topped the civil engineering batch that semester; an uplifting result when it was least expected.

After the college closed for the summer vacation, I visited Bini in her hostel. We went to a movie, but we could not talk as much as I wanted. She had brought along her friend, Golap, and I could not refuse. Golap was her best friend, but to me she was the third wheel.

'I haven't said anything at home yet,' I told Bini briefly as soon as Golap was out of sight for a moment during the intermission.

'Do you foresee any resistance from the elders?' she asked. Our eyes met for the first time, consciously.

'Yes,' I responded, and noticed a hint of uneasiness on her face.

'But I have the confidence that I will be able to influence them,' I added, to alleviate her worries.

I asked if she had said anything to her family, and she hadn't.

'Do you anticipate any concern from your parents?' I asked.

'I am not sure. But my parents like you. They have heard so much about you from Rajuna,' Bini said.

Ah! Rajuna would be able to break the ice between the two families then, I said, and both of us smiled. We paused our conversation as Golap rejoined us.

After the movie, I accompanied Golap and Bini to their hostel. 'I am sure both of you would like to catch up without me being around,' said Golap with a wink, and vanished into the hostel, leaving Bini and me at the gate.

'I have been intending to ask you this. I am elated that you came around, but will you tell me honestly why you were so furious at my proposal in the first place?' I finally asked.

Bini remained silent, but her smile still lured me.

'Can you imagine the agony you caused me by first remaining silent for three months and then with your rejection?' I pushed.

'It was not a rejection!' Bini protested.

'Then?'

'I had always seen you as a friend. I was jolted by your letter. It was not that I do not like you; it is just that I did not know how to react. I still do not know how I will broach the topic of my marriage with my parents.'

'Are you happy?'

'Yes.'

'Are you making a compromise, Bini?'

'Compromise? Do not say that. It is hurtful.'

I did not want to prolong the discussion, so to change the topic, I told her I had a proposal.

'What?' she asked.

'It is important that we inform our parents that we like each other, and urge them not to entertain any other alliance proposals,' I said.

'There are quite a few proposals coming for me already,' she said, blushing.

'It's the same situation at my home too,' I said, enjoying looking at her blushing face.

'Is that the reason you were in a hurry to propose to me?' she asked.

'If you understand that, I will not let the hurt of the past few months linger in my mind,' I said.

After a few seconds of silence, I initiated another thread of conversation.

'I really do not know how everyone at home will react. I normally do not speak much with Nana and Bhaina, except when I need money. I will coax Nuabou and Bou first. But my biggest source of help, and hope, is Rajuna. He has the strongest influence on everyone at home; especially Nana. At this point, I really do not know how to broach the subject with him. I will figure it out during the summer vacations,' I said.

'What can I say? I still do not know what to do. I will tell my parents, but am not sure how they will react,' Bini said, with what appeared to be a confused smile.

'Everything will get sorted out at the right time, I know. I have your consent; that is all I need at this moment,' I said. 'But I have not yet said the most important thing.'

'What?'

'The most important thing before us is to remain focused on our education. It will take a few years, though I don't exactly know how many,' I said.

'Does that mean no more letters, no more meetings?'

'Once you return to the hostel after your summer vacations, I will write you a letter every week. From now on, I will not sweat too much if I do not receive your replies regularly. I already got the answer to the most important question I had,' I said, bidding farewell to her for the moment.

The summer vacation that year was eventful in more than one way: Nuabou and Bhaina were finally blessed with a baby girl named Rosy, and my younger sister Rita passed the high school board exam and was showing off about going to college.

The financial distress at home was far from easing, but I still broached the topic of Bini, softly, to Bou and Nuabou individually, just before leaving for college. Both were confused, yet happy, and promised to keep the topic under wraps for some time at least.

My mind relaxed; it was time to stay focused on the two final semesters and finish the journey in Rourkela on a strong note.

One anecdote from my seventh semester still makes me laugh: we had a sessional paper on irrigation engineering design. For the viva-voce part, our professor Kshitish Ranjan Jena invited Satya and me together. He first asked a question to Satya, who answered correctly. Then it was my turn, and I was able to answer it. He then asked me a second question, which was tough, and I was unable to answer. He asked Satya, who didn't have an answer either. He then asked a rather simple question to Satya, which I still remember: 'what is the unit for permeability of soil?' I still cannot believe that Satya could not answer the question, and it was his bad luck that the same question was passed on to me. 'Metres per second,' I answered, for the easiest goal I had ever scored in my academic or professional career.

One thing I had noticed during those five minutes of viva-voce was that Satya was under a lot of pressure to win. I had a smile on my face irrespective of whether I could answer or not. What would have happened had the situation been reversed? I still would have come second, and that would be no mean achievement. From the situation that day, I had inferred that I would face numerous similar encounters on the career runway, and that I would not want to put myself under undue pressure all along. It is as important to enjoy the journey while staying on course to reach the destination.

Just put the best foot forward and accept the outcome with all humility—this was going to be my mantra going forward.

I was happy with my performance in the seventh semester, and also approached the Graduate Aptitude Test in Engineering (GATE) exam mindfully.

The ritual of writing a letter to Bini every weekend and receiving her reply towards the latter half of the week continued. I was longing to see her after a gap of six months, during the Christmas break.

Paiana was in his final year of masters in agricultural science at the Odisha University of Agriculture and Technology (OUAT), Bhubaneswar. It was time to catch up with him and update him about my decision to marry Bini. Most importantly, I needed a place to crash at night; sharing his room at OUAT was the perfect solution to everything.

On all three days I was there, I promptly reached Bini's hostel around noon: the first day, we went for a movie; the second, we went to Nandankanan Zoological Park; and on the third day, we decided to just sit somewhere inside the campus and chat.

'You probably know by now already; in my entire village, there are no bathrooms, no toilets,' I informed her.

'In my village too, no other family has a bathroom or a toilet,' she replied.

'Yes, but your family has one. Will you be able to manage in my home?' I asked.

'I can manage without a bathroom; managing without a toilet would be awkward, but I will try. One thing I will say though— having a toilet at home is a good thing,' she said.

The Swachh Bharat Mission was at least three decades away from being launched in India, so Bini was definitely ahead of her time.

She noticed that I had dressed in the same pair of pants and shirt on all the three days we met. Apparently, her friends had teased her about this, and she had been embarrassed. 'You probably like this set of clothes a bit too much, don't you?' she asked me on the third day.

'This is the only good set I have,' I answered with a smile. I noticed her expression change; she felt guilty for having asked that question.

One situation I never wanted to face was to complete my engineering degree and sit at home, waiting for a job. I would not want to subject Nana, Bhaina, Bou and Nuabou to a feeling that all the sacrifices they had made for me had gone down the drain.

However, the job situation in the country at the time was bleak. Mechanical, electrical, chemical and metallurgy students at least had options in the private sector and public undertakings, but the prospects in civil engineering, which had been at their peak three years before, were at their worst by the time we would graduate. The state government was the only source of employment, but sadly, two batches of seniors were still on the bench, waiting to be employed. The political situation in the country was also adding to the woes; India was yet to recover from Operation Blue Star, and serving prime minister Indira Gandhi's assassination on 31 October 1984. For me, a semester away from graduation, the prospect of sitting at home for a few years despite an engineering degree from a prestigious institute was petrifying.

Fortunately, the monthly scholarship in master of technology programme just got revised to a thousand rupees per month that year. The eligibility criterion was simply a good GATE score. For reference, at the time, a salary of Rs 1,500 per month was considered 'well-paid'. So, a thousand rupees in monthly scholarship was not a trivial alternative. Add to it the long-term benefit of adding a master's degree to one's resume while waiting for a job, and my road ahead was quite obvious.

I took the GATE exam seriously, and my score was a pleasant surprise. I had been disappointed to miss out on doing B.Tech. at an Indian Institute of Technology, and this was the perfect opportunity to enrol into an M.Tech. and fulfil my desire of studying at an IIT.

In addition to the bleak job placement scenario, I also had a radical thought subconsciously developing within me—having some idea of the typical career and lifestyle of a state government engineer, I had been gradually developing cold feet towards a career in civil engineering.

Poring over the IIT prospectus, I was intrigued by one thing; M.Tech. in aerospace engineering was open to civil engineering B.Tech. graduates. I had a good GATE score, and the possibility of studying that at an IIT felt captivating.

I was nervous that it would be hard for a civil engineering graduate to compete and do well in an aerospace M.Tech. programme, but realized that things had never been easy for me, and I had endured academic challenges with determination and hard work all along. This had developed into one of my best personal attributes, and this was an opportunity to put it to the acid test.

A dream arose from nowhere, that my childhood hobby of making kites would now give way to making airplanes. The intriguing sight of the bird flirting with my kite five years ago flashed before my eyes. In the blink of an eye, I made the decision, and opted for aerospace engineering as my first preference.

I thought if I did have to fall back on civil engineering as my career option, my B.Tech. degree with honours should be good enough. Why would I want an M.Tech. in the same subject? Moreover, if change really is inevitable, why let it be incremental change; why not quantum change? I decided not to include any specialization in civil engineering as my second or third preference.

After the final semester exam, the students bid farewell to each other. I spent a morning in Sushama Nani's house, and an afternoon with Mausa, Mausi, Babu, Samir and Gita, and returned home with my trunk.

An intimation arrived from IIT Kharagpur during the summer vacations. Everyone at home was confused at what I was stepping into, but seeing me happy, they were happy. I had assured them, much to their relief, that the scholarship I was to receive would more than suffice for my tuition fees, lodging and boarding. I met Rajuna and appraised him about my decision to pursue M.Tech. in aerospace engineering at the IIT, and met Bini en route to Kharagpur. Within a few weeks, another significant transition in my student career was complete.

A few of my batchmates in civil engineering with good GATE scores pursued M.Tech. degrees in civil engineering. I was the only one to go off the beaten track.

Was I being overly impulsive? Yes. But my heart was not in a career in civil engineering. I had given it my best shot, and graduated as one of the toppers in the batch, but I longed for change. How long I could remain oblivious to it?

6

IIT KHARAGPUR: WHERE THE DREAM TOOK WING

NEW LOCATION, NEW INSTITUTION, HUGE campus, new programme and opportunities aplenty for self-development and discovering new friends. It was easy to get lost between the department buildings at IIT Kharagpur. Every hall of residence was named after a prominent freedom fighter. I was in Nehru Hall.

One of my seniors from Rourkela, Mahavir Panda, who was pursuing an M.Tech. in civil engineering, was of great help to me during my first few months at the IIT. Another day, I stumbled upon Prashant Mahapatra, a batchmate with whom I had hardly spoken during the four years at the REC. But, at the IIT, we became very good friends. 'When your options are narrow, you seek out, explore deeper and forge friendships,' I thought with a chuckle.

At the REC, at least outside the classrooms, half my batchmates would converse in Odia, the language most familiar to me. At IIT, that was not the case, and I saw it as a huge opportunity. I forced myself to converse in English persistently. A language is best learned not in a classroom, but rather through colloquial conversations; the environment at IIT enabled this significant change. A thousand rupees of scholarship per month had eased monetary constraints, and subscribing to an English daily newspaper and spending half an hour on it helped broaden my vocabulary. I had a batchmate, Om Prakash Prasad, who also came from a civil engineering background, and faced similar challenges as I did. So, we forged a complementary partnership, and soon became good friends.

My one and a half years in IIT were not only about plain hard work, but also an academic adventure. I can hardly recall what I saw outside the campus.

I do recall, vividly, the two annual events inside the IIT Kharagpur campus: the Dahi Handi extravaganza during the Janmashtami festival, and the inter-hostel illumination competition during Diwali. Such events created unique vibes, enabling the hallmates to gel in teams and compete. If I ever have the desire to visit IIT Kharagpur sometimes, I would pick the night of Diwali. It is by far the most spectacular.

The first semester was the hardest. Aircraft structures turned out to be my favourite, as I could build on what I had already learnt during my undergrad degree, but the two other core subjects, aerodynamics and propulsion, were difficult. I ended up with a grade point average of just above seven.

It was time to introspect and make amends. In all the exams I had faced before coming to IIT, there was no certainty that the professor who taught the paper would also set the question paper and grade the paper. Thus, it was always about covering a subject as broadly and deeply as possible, hoping to get some favourable questions. The level of uncertainty was high. But the redeeming factor was that it was the same for every student in the class. Therefore, consistent hard work was the key to success.

Now, at the IIT, the professor who taught the paper set the question paper and also graded it. It was important to remain in the good books of professors—I am not alluding to the need to suck up, but to know their preferences and align with them. Professors are human beings after all; there were some who liked students to reproduce what had been taught in class, while others encouraged independent research and inclusion of aspects not covered in class.

I applied these principles in the second semester. I had a close shave with a 'C' in just one paper, Computational Aerodynamics, but scored 'A' in all others, ensuring a semester GPA of nine. So, there was progress.

Most importantly, I turned out to be the teacher's pet in quite a few papers. In a three-semester programme, one cannot aspire to be a master of all, but can get a firm grip on one broader topic. That is what specialization is supposed to accomplish. I was clearly on a path to specialize in aircraft structures.

'Lighter kites soar higher,' I recalled Nana telling Bhaina while coaching him about building good kites. The same philosophy applies to aircraft and spacecraft too; they always need to be optimized for minimum weight, thereby ensuring maximum fuel efficiency and manoeuvrability.

The final semester was full-blown project work, and I had to get an 'A'. Through the first two semesters, I had won the confidence of B.K. Parida, a professor who was an authority in the area of aero-structures. Fortuitously, he enticed me to a project in fracture mechanics.

'Considering your interest and aptitude in aero-structures, I feel you will like fracture mechanics. Besides, it is an area that has superior job prospects,' he said. What else could I have asked for? I grabbed the opportunity. Apart from getting an 'A', the project work turned out to be the key differentiator in my transition from academics to a professional career.

But it was not straightforward.

In 1987, the year I graduated from IIT Kharagpur, the Indian economy had hit rock bottom. Software companies, which have risen to be the backbone of employment in India since the turn of the millennium, were in their infancy. There were just a handful of private sector firms which had the potential for large-scale employment creation; the main sources of employment, therefore, were the government and public sector undertakings (PSUs). The irony was that with a reasonably high CGPA in aerospace engineering, it was indeed easier to go abroad to pursue higher education with a full scholarship, and possibly secure a career abroad.

But for me, that option was ruled out, as I had to join a job urgently for two reasons: I was waiting to get married to Bini, and I was resolute about supporting my family, which had made unparalleled sacrifices to get me through college. I had a 'dream company', Hindustan Aeronautics Limited (HAL), the only notable firm providing a stable career option for aerospace engineering graduates in India. Its design and development division was situated in the 'air-conditioned' city of Bangalore (now Bengaluru); one needed a light jacket or sweater while venturing out even on summer evenings. 'What could be a better company and city to begin a career in, and to live in?' I mused.

Fortunately, HAL came to IIT Kharagpur that year for campus placement, and since it was the first company to invite aerospace engineering graduates, everyone in the department had applied. But there was a serious problem. Aerospace engineering graduates had the dubious reputation of quitting HAL within a few years to travel abroad for higher studies, so the company was showing a preference for mechanical engineering graduates over aerospace. It was difficult to believe—being an aerospace engineering graduate was a disadvantage in getting selected for a job in an aerospace company.

No one really knew how many freshers HAL would recruit from our institute, but there were around a dozen senior officials in the interview panel. It felt scary.

The beginning of my first ever serious job interview was bumpy. One official asked me to state the assumptions and write down a few complex formulae in aerodynamics and aerostructures. I did alright on stating the assumptions, but didn't remember the formulae. When the panel persisted, I offered to derive one formula on the spot. One official got exasperated, saying, 'You are supposed to remember the formulae, else you would lose time and even make mistakes while deriving them.' But an elderly official among the panel somehow put me at ease by asking a few fundamental questions in my area of interest, fracture mechanics.

But all in all, I thought I was finished. Therefore, I could not believe my eyes that evening, when the names of selected candidates were put up on the notice board. Seeing my name up there, I felt the relief of a lifetime.

Two years had elapsed since the final semester exam in Rourkela. Most of my batchmates with civil engineering degrees were, unfortunately, still cooling their heels at home, waiting for state government job vacancies. I would have been a frontrunner, but instead of waiting, I had utilized the time to develop a parallel career option by adding an M.Tech. degree from an IIT, specializing in an entirely different area, while earning a decent stipend, culminating with a dream job offer in hand. Call it luck or intuition, I had exercised agility in career planning. I had evaded hitting a wall.

Most importantly, I had evaded the most agonizing moments of sitting at home, waiting for a job.

7

IN PURSUIT OF THE DREAM JOB

BEFORE TRAVELING TO BANGALORE, I wanted to spend some quality time conversing with Nuabou. But that didn't happen, and for a good reason—she and Bhaina were blessed with a son, Raja. I left for Bangalore when he was just six days old, and according to the tradition of home births, Nuabou and Raja had to stay confined to the makeshift delivery room for the first ten days. I did sneak a quick look at Raja before leaving.

This was the first journey away from home when the trusty old trunk didn't accompany me, as I had to travel thirty hours in an unreserved train compartment, and didn't know where I was going to stay in Bangalore. After freshening up in an inexpensive lodge, I went to HAL's administrative block, and then shuttled from department to department the entire day, completing joining formalities, including some medical tests.

In those days, the Light Combat Aircraft (LCA, later named HAL Tejas) was being conceived as India's first indigenous defence project, attracting the who's who of top scientists from space programmes across the globe, including NASA. Young engineers from all over the country were joining HAL in their hundreds almost every month. Long story short, I was just a drop in the ocean.

Joining formalities over, I was asked to meet one senior official, and by the time I found my way in front of him, it was almost five in the evening. This was B.S. Srinivasa Rao (fondly called BSSR), the deputy general manager of aircraft design. Here's how the conversation went, to the best of my memory.

'Good evening, Sir, I was asked to meet you.'

'Good evening. Take a seat.'

'Thank you.'

'Do you remember me?'

'Yes, you were in the interview panel that visited the IIT Kharagpur campus.'

'You are right, that is where I saw you. You were quite nervous during the interview, remember? So much so that you began by answering a few fundamental questions wrong. But I liked your confidence when you said that given time, you could derive Westergaard's equations for normal and tangential stresses at a crack-tip. Could you have truly derived them had I granted you the required time?'

'Yes.'

'They are indeed complex, but that doesn't matter. As I said, I truly liked your confidence and approach. It is insane that some people expect students to remember those formulae, sad that there is so much emphasis on what to remember, and so little on how to derive scientific equations from first principles.'

This was my first one-on-one interaction with a senior person outside college, and I was dumbstruck.

Confused, I offered a 'thank you, Sir'.

'I have thought about a nice research problem that will challenge you for an entire year or so. Would you be interested in working on that problem?'

'I would be obliged if I am granted one wish, Sir. All along, I desired to work in core engineering. That is the reason I am excited to have been selected to work on the LCA project. But my goal is to work on computers. Whatever research problem you assign to me will be fine by me, but will it require to be solved using a computer?'

'I noticed your aptitude for computational mechanics during your interview itself. The research problem that I have in mind is all about computational mechanics. Come tomorrow; I will explain.'

That was my first working day in Bangalore. It was close to six o'clock and I was completely exhausted, but still didn't know where I would sleep that night. Rajuna had given me the address of one person from his village, Nanda bhai, whom I had never met before. I enquired where Jayanagar was, as that was his location, and got into a bus.

I could not stop thinking about my conversation with BSSR sir. He had noticed me during the interview and even remembered my responses! Additionally, showing confidence in my ability, he had set aside an ambitious computational research project for me. He had made me feel special. For him, I was not just another drop falling into the ocean. Not only was I working for my dream company, it looked like I'd landed my dream job as well. I was ecstatic.

Unlike in college, where the ecosystem came pretty much preconfigured—a hostel room, a set of batchmates, a curriculum to follow, a set of professors as sources of help, an exam as the exit test—life as a professional in the faraway city of Bangalore was different. Indeed, overwhelming. Developing a mini ecosystem was necessary for survival.

'Do you smoke?' a colleague called Nihar babu asked out of the blue on my second day in office. I was stunned. He revealed later that he was craving for a smoke, and could see the outlines of two cigarettes in the pocket of my white shirt. For him I was the proverbial 'friend in need', and for me, it was the best return on investment I had ever harnessed out of my occasional smoking habit. Sparing just one cigarette, when he really needed it, is how I made my first friend in Bangalore.

Nihar babu invited me to stay with him, and I agreed in the blink of an eye. He had a motorbike, so I got to experience the thrill of riding pillion for the first time. After collecting my briefcase from Nanda bhai's residence, halfway through our return ride, I got the shock of my life when I realized that Nihar babu himself did not have an assured accommodation. I could not stop laughing.

'Why did you ask me to check out from Nanda bhai's residence then?' I asked.

'Come, we will see!' Nihar babu said. He lived as a paying guest, and I adjusted with him for a couple of days, but things did not work out and we were both kicked out. We roamed around on his motorbike, and by evening, found ourselves in a temporary accommodation. Behera bhai, Nihar babu's acquaintance from the Madras Institute of Technology (MIT), came to our rescue. He shared an accommodation with Purohit babu, so there would be four of us, but thankfully, there were two rooms, so it wasn't a problem.

Soon, I was introduced to two other Odia friends, Praveen (popularly known as Patnaik) and Acharya. Both worked in HAL, and shared another accommodation nearby in Marathahalli. That made six of us—all bachelors living close by, working in a big city far from home. We became a team, and had unlimited amounts of fun: I sang, Patnaik showed off his sense of humour and leg-pulling skills, Nihar babu narrated adventures from MIT, while Behera babu, Purohit babu and Acharya shared their life experiences.

Breakfast and lunch during weekdays were not a problem, thanks to HAL's canteen. But roaming around for food every night and during weekends was a problem, especially for me, as I was trying to save some money. I proposed to cook regularly, and though initially everyone was sceptical, we soon gelled. Acharya was the only one who had an LPG gas connection and a stove, so he had to be cajoled first. Nihar babu was in charge of grocery shopping, as he owned a motorbike. As his smoking partner, I used to tag along with him. Behera babu generously let his kitchen be used, while Patnaik loved to wash and cut vegetables, neatly and scientifically, into perfect geometric shapes. Nihar babu, the most innocent among us, used to spiritedly clean all the dishes. I began as assistant chef to Purohit babu, but soon he got busy otherwise, prioritizing the hunt for a life partner over cooking. So, I became the de facto head chef. Apart from eating healthy and spending less, we had developed our own sustainable social ecosystem of working bachelors.

Making friends at work and outside, managing in shared accommodations, and devoting as much time at work as possible were all priorities. But the overarching priority for me was to get married. It had been four years since Bini and I had agreed to walk our future together. Averaging one letter per week, we had already exchanged over two hundred letters each, but we had hardly met. How long could we carry on like pen-friends? None of my colleagues and friends seemed to be in a hurry; they wanted to settle down first: own a house or plot of land, get a cooking gas connection, own a vehicle, build up some savings. The list was endless. All this seemed too much for me. I did not see the need to get 'settled' before getting married; that could continue happening. To my mind, the whole motivation behind marriage is to get unsettled first, explore and reestablish priorities, unlearn and relearn things, undo and redo habits. Plan a family and live a life when curiosity is at its peak. Build a home brick by brick—together, not alone. Thus, I rushed to put in place what I thought was a bare minimum—a small amount of savings to pay as security deposit for renting a house, and then set out for my marriage.

Patnaik was a great companion and source of help during this crucial transition in my life. He accompanied me to a printing press in Shivajinagar to print my wedding invitation, and buy a cot and a kerosene stove. They were small gestures, but big for me at the time. Patnaik had won my heart.

Rajuna was ever-present at every step in the build-up to my wedding. He did not need a formal invitation, but according to custom, I went to meet him in person with the first invitation. Second on my list was someone I had bumped into one day when I was on the verge of starvation—the sweet shop owner at Niali bus stand, who knew I had no money, but had fed me two rasagollas. I had been so shy that let alone thanking him, I hadn't even asked his name. Later, I came to know he was Banka Sahu. No, strike that out. Banka bhai.

On reaching his shop, I presented him with my wedding invitation and asked him to serve two plates of rasagollas. I pleaded with him to share one plate with me, and he appeared confused. So, I recounted what he had done for me ten years ago.

'Banka bhai, allow me to express my gratitude this way today,' I pleaded. After we finished gulping down our sweets, I offered him money, which he refused. But I was determined to pay, and got my way. We chatted for a few minutes—he enquired about my job, about Bangalore and about Bini.

I asked him how come he didn't remember feeding the starving boy those rasagollas ten years ago, and he responded philosophically, 'I don't try to remember every incident, but I do try not to forget some!'

'What do you choose to remember and to forget, Banka bhai?' I asked, intrigued.

'I don't remember the incidents where I helped someone. And I never forget the ones where I was at the receiving end of kindness.'

'Why is that, Banka bhai?'

'It is a very simple philosophy. If I remember every little thing I do for others, I will develop expectations from them. I will remain restless and unhappy till those expectations are met. If I forget them, there are no worries. On the other hand, if someone has helped me, I never forget that. Being grateful is the shortest route to feeling happiness within. That feeling of happiness will continue to inspire me to work harder, and will ensure that I don't forget to reciprocate the kindness I once received from them.'

Being grateful is the shortest route to feeling happiness within—what a simple yet profound truth!

'Why do people forget that, Banka bhai?'

'Some people don't forget, like you didn't. And some people also don't remember, like I didn't!' said the streetside philosopher and guide. I was in awe of him.

'Not many would address me as bhai, but you did. I will surely come for your wedding,' he said.

The rendezvous with Banka bhai made me contemplative on my way back from the shop. Our state of mind and actions are influenced by the things that we remember, not by the things we have long forgotten. We, therefore, must be conscious of the things that we choose to remember and the things that we choose to forget, I reflected.

Our wedding at Bini's home was a small affair—only close relatives and a few of our intimate friends attended. At my home, she was usually surrounded by many people, mostly relatives. No one at my home had said anything or set any expectations, but Bini had her impenetrable ghoonghat (traditional veil) on all the time. The more people tried to catch a glimpse of her face, the stronger she pulled it down firmly. I had never visualized her as such a drama queen; I first saw her face four days after the wedding!

'How have you been feeling over the last four days?' I asked her when we met on the most-awaited night in Odisha tradition, Chauthi Rati.

'The people at your home, I mean our home, are really nice. Everyone, except you!'

'What did I do wrong?' I asked.

'You will know at the right time...' she replied.

'How have you been managing without a toilet and bathroom?'

'I had told you—the bathroom is not a challenge, but the toilet is. Going to open paddy fields felt odd the first time, but slowly, I am getting used to it. Bou and Nani (Nuabou) have been affectionate, and have gone with me. Rita is wonderful. I am being spoiled by a lot of pampering, especially from Bou. You were right, the Hensanaga pond is indeed vast and serene. Taking an early morning dip in it is quite a rejuvenating experience,' Bini said.

But then, when I tried to cajole her into starting the main event of Chauthi Rati, she asked me to shut up and handed out a ruling—'nothing is happening until you construct a toilet in our backyard!'

I gave her a look that said 'blackmailing started already?' and we both cracked up.

Soon after, Bini and I travelled to Bangalore to begin our life together. Over the next few years, many events unfolded, both in my professional and personal life—many expected, some totally unanticipated. I did get to work on an IBM 3090 computer to solve complex engineering problems, developed great friends at work, visited Lalbagh, Cubbon Park, M.G. Road, Brigade Road, Majestic, Commercial Streets and many more attractions in the city; travelled to nearby places like Tipu Sultan Palace, the Brindavan Garden in Mysore, Ooty in Tamil Nadu and Hogenakkal Falls between Tamil Nadu and Karnataka.

The man who had put me on my dream career path, BSSR, retired after a few years, but working with my next boss, M.K. Sreedhar, I made a few significant contributions to the LCA project, published many technical papers in national and international journals, and travelled to quite a few conferences.

Bini turned out to be a relationship builder—apart from deepening my relationships with Patnaik, Nihar babu, Acharya, Behera babu and Purohit babu, she helped expand our social circle to include Biswal bhaina, Mallick bhaina, Sahu bhaina, Satpathy bhaina, Das babu and Mahapatra babu, to name a few. Thanks to my love for singing Odia songs, I got involved, and subsequently took leadership in the Odisha Cultural Association.

Everyone from my family took turns to visit and stay with us in Bangalore. I accompanied all of them to see the Lalbagh Botanical Garden and the Brindavan Garden in Mysore. Our nephew Raja lived with us for a few years, to fulfil our aspiration of educating him in an English medium school. I bought a Bajaj Chetak scooter, a Godrej fridge and a 14-inch black-and-white TV.

The birth of our daughter, Shilu, brought loads of happiness to our entire family. Bou lived with us to help raise Raja and Shilu, and in the meantime, Rita got married and settled down.

Then, Bini joined a middle school as a teacher. Life, in the eyes of the outside world, seemed to be busy and going well. But deep inside, I had mixed feelings about where my life was headed.

One incident made me introspect. After a brief vacation, Bini and I were returning from our hometown, leaving behind our two-year-old Shilu in my village. Upon reaching the Bhubaneswar railway station, we found that our train, the Guwahati-Bangalore Express, was running twenty-four hours late. Instead of returning to our village, we decided to visit a relative's house in Bhubaneswar. It was a bit embarrassing, but we did not have any other choice: there were no options like checking the train status online. Even calling up railway stations could be extremely unreliable; the only way to check was to go to the station physically and ask at the enquiry counter.

After staying for a day in the relative's house, when we got back to the station, we came to know that the train was further delayed by thirty hours. Besides, I was feeling a bit feverish. We did not have much money to rent a hotel, so we hatched a plan: I conspired to look really sick, more than I would normally appear when running a mild temperature, as we approached the station master with a request to kindly allot us a room meant for transit passengers in urgent need. The ploy worked, and we got a room at a significantly concessional rate. Still, it pushed us to the edge, as we had not planned for that one extra day of boarding and lodging. We did board the train the next day, but by the time it reached Vijayawada, we were hardly left with any money, and had at least another twelve hours' journey left to reach Bangalore. Somehow, we managed, skipping one main meal to save five rupees to buy two bus tickets from Bangalore Central railway station to our residence in Marathahalli. By the time we reached our apartment, prepared a pot of khichdi and ate, it was well past midnight.

'Money cannot buy happiness' goes the adage. The real question however is, how much money? Where is the threshold? Preach this adage to someone who skipped a meal in a train to save five rupees for the bus ticket, and you will get one answer.

Ask the same question to someone who has enough money to commute by air to attend a wedding, despite having plenty of time at hand for commuting by train, and you will receive a different answer.

I had been working as an aeronautical engineer in an aircraft design and manufacturing company for over six years, but had not flown in an aircraft. That did not bother me, yet. What troubled me was the fact that I could not afford a comfortable train ride to my hometown when there was an urgent need. Some level of financial stability was essential to lead an inclusive life, and I had to have the money to support and care for my family, I realized.

Bini was naïve; she had never made any demands, assuming that I may not be able to fulfil them. Six years had passed, and I still had not fulfilled her one and only wish—constructing a toilet in my village home. Whenever we visited, she continued to join Bou and Nuabou in the woods, without grumbling. She began her life with me by adjusting her lifestyle; soon adjustment became second nature to her.

When Nana visited us once, he noticed my struggle. 'Our son became an engineer; he is working in a reputed company, apparently. Why is he struggling so much financially?' I could read the question in his eyes.

My maternal uncle once requested me to help his son, my cousin, get a job. In his mind, I was an engineer in a big company in Bangalore, and it should have been rather easy for me to find a job for my cousin. He did not realize that I was just a drop in the ocean, and did not really command much influence in matters like getting someone a job. I did not feel too bad, as my cousin was not very qualified. However, I felt guilty for not being able to provide some funds so that he could at least start a small business of his own.

I wanted to help people. I had travelled some distance as a scrapper, but I had a long journey ahead. I had developed bigger aspirations; I wanted to help many scrappers who had a genuine desire to succeed in life. And that required some financial strength and security.

The government and PSUs back then were outstanding at providing secure jobs in bulk. The pay and benefits in those companies, however, were barely adequate for 'roti, kapda, makaan' (food, clothes, house). Banka bhai's words were providing me constant impetus, as I dreamt of repaying the favours of the many people, within and outside my core family, who had helped me in my student days. I did not want to see Bhaina and Shyama toiling as hard as they used to when I was in college. It was painful to see Nana still working in the paddy fields at the age of sixty-five. I wanted him to slow down and take life easy. I wanted to help our family a bit more financially. Ironically, when I received my first promotion at HAL, it was an increase of Rs 130 on my basic salary. Even if you included the perks and benefits, the monthly salary jumped by just Rs 250—barely enough for dinner with family in a decent restaurant. I was feeling restless; Nuabou's necklace was yet to be brought home. I wanted to fulfil my dream of accompanying Bou to Rameswaram, and to show her the Rama Setu. A dream job in a big aerospace company was not propelling even the smallest of my dreams into flight.

As a student, I had succeeded in turning scarcity into opportunity by devoting more time to studies. As a working professional and a family man, the story was no different. I had devoted substantial time developing my technical and social skills. It was time to monetize those skills.

It was the summer of 1994; Bini and Shilu were visiting our village, leaving me alone in Bangalore for a few months. I noticed an advertisement in the *Deccan Herald*—Tata Consultancy Services (TCS) was recruiting engineers to execute a large contract in the engineering services domain. The pay would be better. I applied, appeared for an interview in Bangalore, and got selected to join its engineering services division in Madras (now Chennai). As soon as I got the offer letter, I resigned from HAL, and then things snowballed quickly. I visited my village to update everyone about my decision, and bring Bini and Shilu back with me to Bangalore. Everyone at home was somewhat apprehensive about quitting a government job to join a private sector company, but they did not have much wisdom to impart to me in these matters, and the fact was that I had already resigned. Bini did not know how to react to this news, but she did what she does best—support my decision with a smile on her face.

After serving my notice in HAL, we moved to Madras. Fortunately, we did not own too many things—all of our belongings failed to fill half of the moving company's smallest available truck. I realized that agility is inversely proportional to baggage.

Bini had to quit her teaching job in Bangalore, and was in two minds about looking for another in Madras. Shilu joined kindergarten as I forayed into another eventful phase of my career.

I vividly remember my first project in TCS: a cluster of conversion projects that none of the so-called youngsters were enthused about. We had hundreds of engineering drawings to be converted from one computer-aided design (CAD) platform to another—a labour-intensive undertaking. To me, it was the grown-ups' version of mugging up the summaries of twenty-nine poems just for twenty marks, without even understanding what I was mugging up.

But I was not going to give up easily. A few weeks into the project, when the tasks appeared utterly monotonous to the entire team, my curiosity incited me to go from 'hard work' to 'smart work'. I began to look for patterns of repetitive tasks within the monotonous conversion algorithm, and identified several automation opportunities. As the automation tools got developed, tested and applied, the output during the conversion process swelled exponentially, while the effort shrunk dramatically.

Productivity is the ratio of output to input. I knew the definition, though I never had a feel for it before leading this conversion project. While measuring productivity as a function of effort, I recalled Rajuna's question, 'what would you get if you divide any number by zero?' My one-time effort on automation had propelled me into such a scenario: significant output with minimal effort, yielding high productivity. This project not only taught me the science and art of the 'feel for numbers', but also handed me one of the finest lessons in my career: however mundane it may seem, any job, if executed with curiosity, perseverance and purpose, can teach a lesson or two, and can yield dream outcomes.

Plus, it can open many new doors of opportunity!

Engineering services was a new domain back in 1995, so TCS had a dearth of experienced people. One good opportunity opened in its Bombay (now Mumbai) branch. I was approached to take a transfer, but we were expecting our second child, and Shilu was also doing well and liked her school. So, I put in a request that I be allowed to travel to Bombay on deputation. The request was accepted without a hitch, and the company also agreed that I could travel—by flight—once a month to see my family. Being a first-of-its-kind project, there were customer escalations, for which I was asked to go to the US for three months, and execute the project at the customer's location.

Bou, living with us then, was the main source of psychological support to Bini for sure, but she was old and did not know the local language. So, we were quite nervous. But TCS never forced me; it was Bini who inspired me to not let the opportunity pass. 'Our doctor has assured us that most likely it would be a normal delivery. Even if you are present, what can you do? God is there for us. Everything will be fine, you just go!' she urged. My younger brother Shyama was summoned to manage the household in my absence, as I boarded my first flight to the US.

By the time I completed the three-month assignment and returned to Madras, our son Ashish was already two months old. To this day, he pokes fun at me, saying 'you like your daughter more than me'. Looking back, one could argue about whether it was wise for me to travel to the US at that juncture, but I was hungry for success. Fortunately, things turned out well. Fortune indeed favoured the brave.

In time, I was given the opportunity to lead the engineering services group in Chennai. Unlike now, when we have perhaps more laptops and desktops than the number of employees in IT companies, at the time there was a dearth of computing resources in TCS. Many of the associates used to come in shifts and execute projects to meet stringent schedules demanded by customers. One day, I went with a proposal to Mahalingam sir, the then head of TCS Chennai, to buy some thirty-odd desktop computers. He gave me an exercise to calculate the revenue generated by my team as well as the cost incurred to generate that revenue, and then present a 'business justification' to him. He would then assess if we were making enough profit from our operation, and then possibly approve my request for procuring desktop computers. I nodded my head and was about to leave his office at 185, Lloyds Road, when he stopped me, saying, 'I am not sure if you have understood the complexity of the exercise. The cost incurred must include cost-to-company (CTC) of all engineers on your team, the cost of computers, printers, building, power, water, lunch subsidy, and cost of marketing. I mean, try to get a handle on the full loaded cost.'

I nodded again, and on my way back, thought I'd better read a finance book first. Nonetheless, I completed the exercise and returned to him again with my request. That was the typical grind I used to go through with Mahalingam sir, but today, I do not regret it. Whatever I am today is all because of the learnings from those difficult experiences. He taught me everything about what the management gurus preach as 'frugal leadership'.

Barely after a year of leading the engineering services group in Chennai, I was chosen to travel for a long-term assignment as the business relationship manager (BRM) to the United States. With frequent changes in assignments, I was getting a feeling of being kicked like a football, but to be honest, I was getting used to it, and with time, I was realizing its brighter side. Maximum learning happens when taking up a new job, and I had found myself on a path of accelerated learning.

I distinctly remember 21 January 1998, when I landed in the US with Bini and our two little kids. The temperature difference between Chennai and Schenectady, New York, was close to a hundred degrees Fahrenheit. Working with the US clients, I was getting used to several cultural shocks; this time, my family and I experienced thermal shock too!

My role as a BRM was going great when TCS and its biggest customer at the time, General Electric (GE), reached an agreement to form a joint venture company in Bangalore. My name was proposed as the leader of the company. Shilu was settling down in her lower primary school, Ashish was beginning to speak short yet complete sentences, I was just starting to enjoy long drives to Niagara Falls, Manhattan, Lake George and Lake Placid, and Bini had just finished unpacking and arranging our rental apartment to her satisfaction in the city of Niskayuna, New York. So, we repacked our bags, uprooted ourselves again, and returned to commence our second innings in Bangalore.

Bini, who hardly ever questioned my decisions, especially on matters related to my career, made a compelling argument on this occasion.

'Are you not reacting too impulsively this time?' she asked. 'We have just settled down, your job is financially rewarding, Shilu is doing well in her school and Ashish seems to have adjusted very well to the new environment. You seem to be doing well. And most importantly, you seem to be enjoying this role. You have earned it. It is time for you to reap the benefits of your hard work. Instead, why would you opt to unsettle and scramble around again?'

But I replied that I had no option to say no. 'Mr Ramadorai, the CEO and MD of TCS, has himself proposed my name. I have always believed that my potential is best known to my superiors, especially those who observe me closely. In high school, it was Rajuna; at engineering college, it was professors Jena and then Parida; at HAL, it was BSSR sir, and now it is Ramadorai sir. Don't you see a pattern? All I do is trust their gut instinct, grab the opportunity, and give my best. I strive consciously not to let them down. It works magically!'

Bini was still not convinced, so I had to give an emotional flavour to my appeal.

'As a student, the only aspiration I had was to land a job. Any job. Now I not only have a job, but also a series of assignments one after the other. With the change of assignments, we are moving to places and broadening our exposure. I am happy, aren't you?'

Bini could no longer overlook my passionate plea. 'What are we waiting for then? Let us begin our packing!' I thought she was being sarcastic, but I took it with a smile.

8

THE LEADERSHIP JOURNEY

U PON REACHING BANGALORE, WE LIVED at the TCS guest house for a few weeks, and soon finalized a rental house. Bini got busy with putting Shilu in a school, buying furniture, arranging the house, managing the household and reconnecting with old friends. Meanwhile, I got engrossed in my new assignment.

The thought that had inspired me to take up the leadership role of the joint venture in Bangalore was that I dreamt of growth in multiple dimensions: the experience of starting a new organization, growing team capability, building credibility with both stakeholder organizations, the potential of creating opportunities for large scale employment, learning and applying new skills, personal growth, and in the process, enabling the growth of many colleagues. I may not be an entrepreneur by definition, but thanks to this assignment, I could learn and nurture my entrepreneurial skills.

All these dreams were unfolded in due time, rather at an accelerated pace. The new company, named Engineering Analysis Centre of Excellence (EACoE) Pvt. Ltd, was established on the tenth floor of the ITPL Innovator Tower in Whitefield. After the ribbon-cutting ceremony with Corbett Caudill (VP Engineering, GE Aviation), in the presence of N. Chandrasekaran and Ravi Goel (alternate directors of the JV representing TCS and GE respectively), Mr Ramadorai (CEO and MD of TCS) handed over the scissors to me, and said, 'From now on, it is your baby.' I felt that was the simplest, most effective way to empower people, and I was determined to give my best and fulfil the responsibility entrusted to me.

The right people at the helm will ensure that the right process gets developed and followed. The converse, however, may not be true. In the 'people versus process' conundrum, I believed in placing my bets on people.

'When you hire people that are smarter than you are, you prove you are smarter than they are' states a quote attributed to R.H. Grant. I did not have to prove I was smarter than anyone, but I certainly believed in the first part of the quote, so I made sure to personally interview and approve the selection of the first two hundred employees of EACoE.

'Do you have any question that I could help clarify?' I would ask before concluding my interaction with every prospective employee.

In response, one of the prospective employees, B. Baskaran, asked me, 'What do you see as the future of this new JV company?'

'TCS and GE: two world-class organizations have joined hands. They have entrusted me with a playbook that begins with an abstract organization structure and business plan. But the rest of the book is empty. We would co-author the playbook, scripting our journey of successes and learning from failures, leaving behind the legacy of developing a world-class engineering organization from scratch. Does it excite you, Baskaran? If it does, come, join the team. We will do it together,' I told him.

I had forgotten about this, but Baskaran reminded me of my words a few years later, in a different context. He admitted he had fallen for my answer, and for the company, which was yet to be built.

Based on the personal interest shown by individuals in their interviews, and my own intuition, I handpicked a few as potential fits to important leadership roles. Some worked out and some didn't, but with time, the expanded leadership team of EACoE pretty much emerged from the list of those first two hundred employees.

A few colleagues played selfless and sedulous roles in getting EACoE off the ground. Baskaran was the one I ran to for help while setting up the initial computing infrastructure. Soon, I placed my bets on a young engineer, Happy Mohanty—like his name suggested, he was always smiling. Working under the supervision of Baskaran, he turned out to be quite a responsible leader, capable of handling independent responsibility.

General Electric was big on 'Six Sigma' quality processes, while TCS believed in the Software Development Capability Maturity Model (CMM) at the time. I was on the lookout for a leader who could dig into and incorporate the best of both practices into the EACoE's quality procedures. My mind turned to Amulya, my batchmate at REC Rourkela, who had wholeheartedly and indefatigably given me bicycle rides to the hospital when I was in dire need. He had completed his PhD from IIT Chennai, and I thought he could be tried and groomed to execute the role. Over a phone call, I enticed him and prepared him for an independent assessment by the GE leadership. He came out with flying colours.

Four of my other TCS colleagues—Krishna, Prasan, Mallika and Nisha—had been deputed to EACoE to partner with me in running the enabling functions of human resources, finance and office administration. These were the seven colleagues with whom I spent numerous hours during the formative stages of the EACoE, and I will forever remain indebted to them.

I had made a conscious effort to emulate the best practices from both the parent organizations and implement them in EACoE. Running the operation with a frugal mindset, yet with the warmth of running a joint family, and focusing on recruiting a large number of young talent from their institute campus were practices adopted from TCS. Focusing on the leadership pipeline, performance management, annual business and succession planning, and communication flow down were prevalent in GE, but were considered too radical in the Indian context. Nevertheless, they were all implemented.

Talking about running an organization with the warmth of a family, I still laugh thinking about this incident from 2000. The EACoE was in its infancy, yet to establish its own campus recruitment programme. With a fine gesture, TCS had offered to depute a good number of freshers to EACoE. The freshers had completed TCS's flagship initial learning program (ILP) and were ready to be deployed into projects. One evening, I received a phone call from one such fresher, Laxmi Gunupudi. After completing her ILP in Thiruvananthapuram, she had just arrived at Bangalore Central railway station to join EACoE, and wanted to know where her accommodation was arranged. I had no idea, nor did I know of another person who could be of immediate help. It was a bit late in the evening, and I did not want Laxmi to feel unwelcome. More so, I was concerned about her safety. Therefore, I asked her to come over to my home, assuring her that something could be figured out the next morning. There was silence at her end; I understood her dilemma. 'I live with my wife and two children. You do not have to worry, Laxmi. I realize that it is an unusual invitation; it is only because I do not know whether your accommodation has been arranged or not, and I do not want you to get stranded in an unfamiliar city,' I said. 'Sir, I contacted you as my joining letter had your name and phone number. Please do not worry. Thank you for the invitation. I have many close friends and relatives in Bangalore. I will stay with one of them and take a bus to the office tomorrow,' she said, while acknowledging my gesture.

My interaction with Laxmi that evening was not a one-off— that is how EACoE functioned. Whatever was felt to be right was followed first; rules and procedures were written next.

It feels nostalgic to recall EACoEtsav, where employees and their families participated and performed on stage to thunderous applause from the audience. I used to sing one song every year, not to show off my singing talent, but to send a soft message that having fun in the company of colleagues was as much encouraged as doing great work for the customers.

After the inaugural edition of EACoEtsav, Laxmi stopped by my office holding a packet. I asked her to take a seat. 'Sir, I observed you during the family day event yesterday, and I observed ma'am and your children too. And I was recalling my first ever conversation with you from the railway station,' she said, and we exchanged a smile.

She also said, 'I really liked your singing, but I feel your voice would be better suited to rendering ghazals by Jagjit Singh ji.'

What else could I say, other than murmuring a simple 'thank you'? Laxmi opened the packet on her way out, handing over a cassette, saying, 'Please accept this simple gift from me.' It was the album *Saher* by Jagjit Singh. I listened to the album on my way back home the same evening. From that day onward, I was not just Pranab Kishore Patnaik's disciple, I was Jagjit Singh's too.

Over the next one year, the EACoE grew from strength to strength. It earned the recognition of being a jewel in the crown for both GE and TCS. Its board meetings ran smoothly; cooperation and chemistry between the board of directors was a treat to the eyes; empowerment was real. I was encouraged to implement all ideas that were envisioned as best for EACoE; I believe I had earned it. During the inaugural Engineering Recognition Day (ERD) event, it was heartening to see the board members from both the parent organizations—Ramadorai and Chandrasekaran from TCS, and Caudill and Goel from GE—recognizing budding engineers who had excelled.

After two years of operating in the ITPL building, the EACoE eventually moved into the magnificent John F. Welch Technology Centre (JFWTC) campus. From the beginning, I had made a conscious effort for EACoE to remain aligned with the larger JFWTC. At the same time, I was also mindful of it creating its own oeuvre. As the largest subset of the vast JFWTC, EACoE had developed the reputation of being the most grounded, yet innovative and growing organization, where every employee was aligned with the mindset that we were building an organization brick by brick, together. It was this feeling of belonging that set EACoE apart, propelling it to be a talent magnet among the engineering design companies at the time.

I recall the emotions when GE decided to buy out TCS's stake to make EACoE its wholly owned subsidiary. It was not easy—some employees, including me, had the option to choose between TCS and GE. Both were among the best-in-class companies, so it was difficult to choose one over the other. But I had to choose one, and it was by far the toughest decision in my career. As per the joint venture agreement, more than ninety percent of my colleagues were going to move to GE. I wanted to ensure a feeling of security to the larger team of colleagues, and so head won over heart—I chose GE. I recall that evening, when I returned after conveying my decision to Mr Ramadorai and Mr Chandrasekaran at the TCS headquarters at the Air India Building in Nariman Point, Mumbai. I was in tears.

I also vividly remember Mr Chandrasekaran, with his trademark gesture of wrapping one arm around my shoulder, consoling and assuring me, 'Do not worry, consider returning to TCS after a few years, if you want to.' It felt like receiving a rain check—an assurance of association, love and trust, wrapped in an envelope, to be opened at an opportune moment. The bridge was not burnt, but rather reinforced with genuine good feelings about each other.

My new role at GE soon led to new experiences and realizations. Every organization goes through challenges: I recall one of the divisions of GE going through significant team compression. It was a mammoth exercise to redeploy the affected engineers, but I was also committed to walk the path with the team in difficult times. Renewing my connections, several engineers found their new home in TCS, and many others got absorbed into other divisions within GE. 'All the affected engineers could be redeployed, except two; we have to do something for them,' urged Aarif, the HR leader at the time. I actually liked his employee advocacy. Fortunately, both those employees were also trying their best on their own—one left to pursue his PhD at IIT Bombay, while the other found an okay job in another company. Both felt sad when they left EACoE, and I could empathize with them. I promised to get back to them whenever a growth opportunity knocked at the door. And when it did, those two engineers were among the first to receive a 'come back' call. While the one pursuing his PhD stuck to it, the other did return, and is still with GE at JFWTC, Bengaluru. His name is C.K. Hari.

Like humans, organizations also evolve with time. I recall how we used to work as a team to create and communicate the annual ERD 'theme', to build focus and provide the much-needed impetus as we moved from one year to the next. Articulation of vision and strategy to create a shared need is important for organizational development. Such vision and strategy articulated through the annual ERD theme served as the binding glue for employee engagement.

In the beginning, the focus was on quality and productivity. The theme for the inaugural ERD year, therefore, was 'Operational Excellence through Six Sigma and Digitization'. Soon, the focus turned to building technology skills of employees—the theme of the ERD during one particular year was 'moving up the value chain through technology ownership'. With its focus on the environment, GE had been committed to developing aircraft engines and power turbines with minimum thresholds of emission and noise, so the ERD theme during one of those years was 'competitive edge through safe and eco-friendly technology products'. The focus gradually turned to innovation and growth, which was reflected in the ERD theme 'curious minds: driving product innovation and growth'.

Defining the growth agenda for an organization is relatively straightforward when measured in terms of revenue or market share, whereas attempting the same for an engineering design organization is not that easy. I had conceptualized an interdependent 'product-technology-process' framework to explain the growth agenda, and to enable workplace employee engagement. For a product organization to grow, it must have market leading products, and for that, products must be designed using advanced technology, ensuring speed to market through simplified processes.

It is imperative that each employee in the organization plays a key role in the product-technology-process ecosystem.

This framework, articulated with a simple visual, resonated well and galvanized the entire workforce.

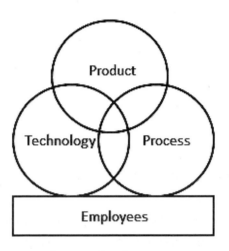

**Product-Technology-Process
framework for enabling growth**

The ERD theme that year was also crafted to reflect this framework—'unfolding minds: fuelling growth through world class products built on innovating technology and simplified processes'.

EACoEtsav, as the annual social funfair, provided an opportunity to the employees and their families to showcase cultural talent. Likewise, the ERD provided the platform to the talented employees to showcase and compete for their technical talent. Two leaders, Maria Sundaram and Alok Nanda, with their hard work and perseverance, had distinguished themselves by leading the charge while organizing the annual ERD events, showing significant promise to grow into much larger organizational roles in the future.

To complement the in-house talent, occasionally, I seek out external collaboration for branding internal business events. One such collaboration was with Maya Chandra. I have no remembrance of how I met her. A freelancing one-woman army then, and now the proprietor of 'Maya Films'; she quickly grasped our technology realm, translated and communicated the ERD theme through a creative and compelling three-minutes video film. She did it year after year, setting new benchmark in quality and impact. Every year I learnt a thing or two from my interaction with her in regard to creativity and imagination.

While the theme of the annual ERD events was being thoughtfully conceived to reflect the alignment and renewal of focus of the subsidiary organization to keep pace with the global organization, I had made it a point to focus on developing an internal pipeline of leaders. I lived by the philosphy that the 'fastest way to grow an organization is to grow its people first'. Training was important, but even more so, it was necessary to create a growth-enabling organizational structure, create leadership opportunities, and push employees with leadership potential to grow into those roles. I was pushed into such roles by my sponsors and well-wishers in the past, time and again. I used to realize it ex post facto, after falling to the ground and rising a few times, and it was fun. It was now my turn to experiment and oversee the development and growth of leaders in my team.

While grooming leaders, the practice established by Kaka to enable me and Sanjunani to cross the hot sand bed of the river in my childhood served as a guiding principle—it was important for me to develop much-needed empathy towards the prospective leaders, and creating leadership roles and walking the first few steps with them was the way to do it. It was then a matter of giving them time, allowing them to learn from their own experiences and grow into those roles. After a while, the enthusiastic new leader was ready to leave me behind and run ahead. That was the time, for me, to stop and cheer, and look for the next one.

Leadership lessons also came from unexpected experiences, like the flower show at the Lalbagh Botanical Garden in Bangalore on India's Independence Day (15 August) every year. Bini and I had visited it as newlyweds and quite enjoyed it; I thought it would be more enjoyable with kids around, and so, after a gap of a decade, I stopped by a second time. On this occasion, the flower show was enjoyable until I entered a section that exhibited a wide variety of bonsai plants. Somehow, I was never a fan of the concept. Would I like to see my children grow as dwarfs? If not, why take a beautiful plant and restrict the supply of nutrients and water, forcing it just to survive as a bonsai plant? If it could speak, would it express happiness over its exposition at a botanical garden?

I followed this analogy while working with the leaders on my team—I created an enabling environment for them to grow, and got out of their way.

'One does not necessarily have to be a people-manager to grow faster in career; employees could grow exponentially by being strong technical leaders too'—I believed in this philosophy. So I obsessively championed 'technical career path' in EACoE, and made sure that one has to excel in making technical contributions first before aspiring to be a leader of people. While leaders like Maria, Alok, Ajit, Vaira and Jaswinder held proven attributes of growing as organizational leaders, leaders like Atul, Sundar, Uma Maheswari, Baskaran, Asim and Hiranmay exhibited stronger promises in technology leadership. Then there were budding talents at every layer of the organization pyramid, who had shown glimpses of their leadership potential. I knew they all would grow up to be super achievers one day. It was just a matter of time.

One of the many skills I learnt personally while working in the JFWTC, and tried to gain mastery at, was mass communication. I had observed a very senior leader holding a piece of paper, reading out key points during an all-employee meeting; not just once, but every time he was slated to go on the podium, even when his speech would barely last one minute. Employees used to get bored listening to him, so his meetings were not well-attended. Speaking to a piece of paper or a slide is something I was not enthused about, I realized, sitting in the audience. So, I made sure to write down key points and messages, memorize them thoroughly, practice a few times, and deliver them passionately, like I had done to win the high school debate competition. It didn't remain a practice for long; soon it became part of my personality. As a leader, it was worth the time and effort to win the hearts and commitment of employees, and mass communication was the most effective enabler.

I laid emphasis on and paid personal attention to rewards and recognition. As a child, I had been amused by the folklore of the squirrel being recognized by Lord Rama. No contribution is small if it's wholehearted, the story constantly reminded me, as I coaxed leaders to go overboard in rewarding their teams. 'If there is one red item on "actual against budgeted" tracking for your teams, let it be rewards and recognition' was my message to leaders—it was the key enabler for building this culture at the EACoE.

After its amalgamation into the JFWTC, the EACoE was renamed Bangalore Engineering Centre (BEC), and it continued to grow with GE's aviation and energy businesses, subsequently expanding to include the oil and gas as well as water businesses. Soon, the engineering teams in Hyderabad and Mumbai were brought under my purview, and the broader team was named India

Engineering Centre. During this growth phase, the sponsorship of GE Global Engineering leaders like Rick Stanley, Vic Abate, Jeanne Rosario and Mohammad Ehteshami will forever be memorable to me. The mentorship of Guillermo Wille, the managing director of JFWTC, and the partnership and camaraderie with Aarif Aziz, Menka Rai, Leena Sahijwani and Rohit Thakur, my close colleagues from human resources, and Archana Handa and Vikram Kanth, communication specialists, will never be forgotten.

After the first four years of operation, we faced a war for talent. Attrition was alarming, so to curb it, I once took my direct staff and the HR partner at that time (Menka) to an offsite event. In an informal and quiet ambience, we worked out a large-scale salary revision plan. When it was time to send the proposal to the senior leadership for approval, Menka said, 'I will go to the temple and offer prayers'.

Once approved, the revised salary structure did help a bit, but the war continued. After three years, I had to execute another salary revision exercise. Menka had already moved on to the UK, so this time, it was the turn of the next HR leader, Leena. To my pleasant surprise, Leena also offered prayers that the proposal would get approved.

If anyone asks me what the single most important attribute of an HR professional is, without batting an eyelid, I would say employee advocacy. I saw this attribute in Aarif, Menka and Leena; at a very young age, they prayed more for their employees, and less for themselves.

Many of my colleagues from the JFWTC fondly recall and remind me about my ritual of holding one-on-one personal conversations. Product-technology-process discussions used to happen in conference rooms, but sensitive and people-related issues were best discussed in informal, benign settings. Throughout my career, I never carried lunch from home, always preferring to eat in the canteen, with the simple intention of observing and giving inputs on food quality to the canteen administration directly, rather than being judgmental and relying on the grapevine. While holding conversations with younger colleagues, I preferred to grab a corner table in JFWTC cafeteria, while to discuss private and serious topics with senior leadership, I preferred taking a tea break.

One day, a younger colleague observed me patiently over lunch. I had not picked up a spoon that day, and scooping out the last few grains of rice using a fork was quite a challenge. But I would not give up; I finally picked them up using my fingers. Intrigued, the colleague asked about it, and I could not help but narrate the story of how my father had made me pick up and eat every single grain of rice from the mud floor. I have narrated the same story to a few other colleagues at different assignments and different times; most of them have been influenced by how that incident at a tender age had imbibed in me the virtue of not wasting food ever—at home, or in the canteen, or at a restaurant.

I had developed an odd habit of adding a small quantity of sugar to my tea or coffee cup and leaving it unstirred, as I kept sipping it in a leisurely manner. One of my staff members, Pravin Gali, had been noticing this for quite some time, and asked me about it.

'Weird, isn't it?' I said with a chuckle, tickling his curiosity. Then I narrated the story from Ravenshaw College, where rural folks like me relied on flattened rice for breakfast. The chivda was home-grown, but sugar had to be purchased, so I would gulp down a few scoops of just the soaked chivda before adding any sugar. This would ensure that the final few scoops were sweet enough to leave me with a good taste in the mouth. Similarly, if you are really craving for tea, unsweetened tea would feel pretty good too. With the lone sugar cube at the bottom, the tea would get sweeter as you went through it. This way, you would start with the taste of fresh tea and end with the taste of honey, and so, you wouldn't bother to remember how the first sip felt.

I approached life like that too. Many people say the first impression is the last impression, but to me, the last impression is the lasting impression. It is a general tendency to take the easy route and focus on making a good first impression, but building relationships and getting people on your side is a long journey, and first impressions may be forgotten.

We had a well-equipped pantry serving great tea and coffee, and I did enjoy one-on-one conversation with my staff while holding a cup. However, I often preferred to walk to a roadside tea stall just outside the JFWTC entrance. I liked the roadside tea as it reminded me of my life's journey; plus it was boiled with ginger roots and customized to individual tastes. It was also served hot in a smaller quantity at a very affordable price of only two rupees. Finally, the fourth reason was purely human—one scrapper supporting another scrapper in earning his or her living. My staff members knew this fourth reason, so before I left Bangalore for my next assignment, they bade farewell to me with a gift—a picture of them sipping tea with me outside the roadside tea stall.

Empathy, as an attribute, extended beyond life at work, to the lives of staff members at home.

One particular morning, we had a review meeting set up, but I received an email from Anbarasu the previous night, stating that his five-year-old daughter, Deepthi, was running a fever. He requested that we shift the review to the afternoon as he would probably have to take her to a doctor in the morning. I had replied something to the effect 'sorry to hear that our beautiful Deepthi is running a fever. Please take her to the doctor. We can do the review in the afternoon, or even a couple of days later. Tell her that I really like her smile and long hair'.

Five minutes later, Anbarasu sent another email, saying 'now her fever is gone!'

Apparently, Deepthi had been sitting on his lap when we were exchanging emails. 'Damodar Uncle really thinks I am beautiful? Does he really like my smile and hair? You never told me this before!' she had interrogated him, and as punishment, she had asked him to read out my e-mail to her over and over again.

Thinking back on it, I believe the email to Anbarasu had four elements of an empathetic conversation, which I call the 'PACT of small talk'—it was Personalized and Appropriate to the person it was intended for—Deepthi; it raised Curiosity in the mind of the recipient; and it was Timely. It is a good way to articulate empathy, at work or in life beyond it.

Like any great company, GE had the innate interest in community development, even amid its focus on product and technology innovation and building a winning team. Donating computers, as well as funding and teaching underprivileged children in schools and organizations were prevalent practices. I wanted to make a humble beginning and oversee its impact at the grassroot level.

One afternoon, my colleague Rajashekhar Malur and I were driving around in the Whitefield area, when we saw the Government Lower Primary School in Pattandur, Agrahara. The school primarily catered to children of construction workers who had migrated in large numbers to Whitefield, which was just booming with numerous MNCs opening their software development centres. But the plight of the children was miserable—the school did not have a compound wall, toilets or potable water. It had only two teachers in total for handling all children up to class five.

My mind flashed back to my own village school, where we had one teacher taking care of children up to class three. 'Out-of-warranty old computers, books, or for that matter, some funding are not the kind of help the school really needs. What it needs is some meaningful assistance in teaching, and basic sanitation for children,' I said, and Raj and I discussed possible opportunities on our drive back.

I recall floating the idea in a well-attended meeting of all employees held in the JFWTC canteen over an informal tea break. Several employees came forward to create a volunteer group under the name EISA (Elfun Initiative for School in Agrahara). 'EISA' is a homonym of a Hindi word that means 'just like that'; something that could be taken to mean no vested interests. Project EISA showed how, in a few years, our volunteers could uplift a school from a precarious situation to a level where it set a benchmark in primary education.

We got started on both the issues—sanitation and education—simultaneously. First, a compound wall and a few toilets were constructed. All toilets were connected to water and sewerage lines, and two potable drinking water taps were also provided. We sponsored a car to have three of our employee-volunteers commute to the school every day for an hour to join the two regular teachers, so that at least for one full hour, all the five classes in the school would run without any noise. The three volunteers would also assign enough homework so that the children remained busy after they left the school. The undertaking was labour-intensive and not easy to sustain in the long run, but we persisted anyway.

The selfless volunteering efforts paid rich dividends, as several of the children cleared the state-run Navodaya Exam to get free admission to English Medium Boarding Schools. One of my most gratifying moments was to see two of the girls, Priyanka and Soniya, clearing the state-run Joint Entrance Examination and studying engineering.

As a company, GE in those days was known for its people practices. The investment in people development was second to none. I humbly acknowledge the importance the company had entrusted in me by inviting me to the coveted John F. Welch Leadership Development Center in Crotonville, New York, to undergo several senior leadership programmes at regular intervals, and also, to its annual global leadership meeting (GLM) held at Boca Raton Holiday Resort, West Palm Beach, Florida. I also fondly remember receiving the coveted 'Capture Their Hearts' award at the 2004 GE Aviation Leaders Day event for excellence in people leadership.

In February 2007, the Chief Human Resources Officer (CHRO) of GE, John Lynch, was visiting JFWTC, Bangalore. I was directed to pick him up from the Leela Palace hotel.

I was given a heads-up earlier by Sharon Daley, the CHRO of GE Energy, and Rick Stanley, the Vice President and Leader of GE Energy Global Engineering, but I never thought things could be so informal.

John Lynch dragged me into a serious conversation on my career, without causing even a hint of anxiety. In any case, I was a captive audience; I could not run away. The next day, the vice-chairman of GE, John Rice, visited the JFWTC, and in an all-employee meeting, announced my elevation to the Senior Executive Band in GE. The announcement was met with thunderous applause, and I was called upon to speak a few words. I remember searching for words, but have absolutely no memory of what I said. Instead, I recall the look in the eyes of the entire audience, especially my direct staff. I felt for a moment as if all of them had been praying that I receive this recognition.

It took some time to sink in—I was the first engineering leader outside of the US to have been promoted to the Senior Executive Band in GE globally. With my elevation that day, I am sure I had kindled hope in many young minds at the JFWTC that day.

9

FATHERHOOD

ASWEHAVEESTABLISHED, I was not born with a silver spoon in my mouth. But my children were born into relatively easier circumstances. I did not make a conscious attempt to provide them with a privileged upbringing, but I certainly didn't want them to grow as another generation of scrappers.

It is not because I regret my own journey; indeed, had I been from a privileged background, I would never have seen life through as wide a lens as I did. And, if evolution is transformation from the beginning to the current state, I am quite happy with my own evolution. The fact, however, remains that my journey was always on a slippery path, with quite a few 'if-then-else' loops and uncertainties along the way. I also wanted my children to evolve, but from a different starting point—by drawing from the resources and wisdom they had access to. I certainly wanted to see them stand on their own feet as self-assured adults.

When Shilu was about two years old, she experienced a short spell of illness—a urinary tract infection (UTI). She was in agony every time she went to the bathroom. But the doctor had advised more fluids, and the young child had understood that doing that would make her go more frequently, so, when Bini tried to make her drink more water, she came up with all kinds of excuses. Bini found it quite tricky, so the responsibility of handling the situation was passed on to me. I tricked Shilu into drinking butter milk, tender coconut water, sugarcane juice and fruit juice, saying they would not make her go as much as plain water would. But when I tried to take her to the bathroom more often, she realized my trick, and resisted out of fear. I discovered this when she accidentally peed on me a couple of times and cried out in pain. Seeing her suffering, my eyes moistened too, noticing which, she would force herself to stop crying. A two-year-old child, and she had begun associating my tears with her pain. On one occasion, after making her drink a lot of water, I successfully cajoled her into going to the bathroom with me. I noticed tears rolling down as she strained, but she tried her best to put on a smile, saying, 'Daddy, this time it didn't hurt!' She was lying, trying to hide her pain to comfort me.

She recovered by the same evening, but those emotional moments were imprinted in my mind, giving rise to an irreversible belief: an unspoken language pronounces the unique chemistry between parent and child, which needs to be decoded and grasped implicitly.

My journey as a father was as challenging, and therefore as fulfilling, as the one as a professional. Like most others, we learnt parenting on the fly. I came to understand that parenting cannot be delegated even to one's spouse, as fatherhood and motherhood are two faces of the same coin. They must complement each other, else children will receive conflicting messages. Parenting cannot be postponed either; it must be an integral part of day-to-day life.

Shilu exhibited extroversion, and was a standout among the children at her age. Ashish was different; quite active as a child, and though not as voluble as kids of his age, his comprehension and choice of words were remarkable. However, in kindergarten, we noticed him showing symptoms of alphabet reversals. He would write and pronounce 'b' as 'd' and 'q' as 'p'. I was a workaholic, and my wife was quite busy with her daily chores, so we failed to recognize it early on—he was dyslexic. We thought he would grow out of it, but one day, he started crying before boarding the school bus. He said he was being ridiculed by his friends, and even his teacher showed no sympathy. In that instant, I called in for a half-day's leave and went to meet his schoolteacher and principal.

The principal, Mrs Hemachandani, was a seasoned educationist. 'Your child is reversing alphabets because of slow brain-hand coordination,' she said. Then, after a pause, she continued, 'If you throw a ball at him, he would be confused whether to catch the ball in his right hand or the left.'

I too had noticed this, and had been puzzled.

'What can be done?' I asked.

'Observe him carefully, spend time with him. Engage in activities that will force him to use his hand-eye coordination skills. To make it easy for him, throw the ball clearly to his left or right. If he drops the ball, don't discourage him, keep engaging with him instead. Let him not only grow in height and weight, but in confidence as well,' she said.

The meeting was a wake-up call; we began spending more time with our son. We decided that my wife would help him with studies, and I would play different kinds of sports with him. Our living room furniture was rearranged to make room for playing cricket. I assumed the role of the bowler as Ashish batted, and occasionally, to break the monotony, we would reverse roles as well.

Seeing him struggle, I asked one day, 'Baba, would you try batting left-handed?'

'Sure Daddy, let me try,' Ashish replied. He found it natural and more comfortable, and I tasted my first success as a coach. We did not own a TV at home, but we visited my brother-in-law's house to watch interesting cricket matches, especially when India played Australia. At the time, both teams had prolific left-handed batsmen in Sourav Ganguly and Adam Gilchrist, and I wanted Ashish to learn from their styles and emulate them.

To improve his confidence and competitiveness, we soon started playing matches. We bowled twenty-five deliveries to each other every day, and whoever scored more won the day. I would occasionally lose to him intentionally, by a narrow margin, to boost his confidence and keep him interested. But the next day, I made sure to score more runs so that he could improve.

Ashish had a marked weakness—the fear of losing. He would get upset, especially when I won a game by a narrow margin. One day, he needed to score four off the last delivery, and won the game by driving it for four. But after rejoicing for a moment, he started crying, surprising me. He then explained why. 'You bowled a loose delivery intentionally to make me win! If you do that, how will I improve my game?' I chuckled as I gave him a hug. He did not know that cricket was just the medium; my real motive was to let him taste success and boost his confidence to face real life ahead. And I could see that he was on the right path.

I realized that Ashish would soon grow beyond my abilities as a coach. Sadanand Viswanath, the famous wicketkeeper-batsman from India's 1985 Benson & Hedges World Championship of Cricket triumph in Australia, was running a summer coaching camp in the neighbouring National Aerospace Laboratory (NAL) campus ground in Bangalore. I enrolled Ashish in the camp, and while he enjoyed the practice, the one-kilometre walk to the ground was a struggle. One morning we were late, so I carried his cricket kit and asked him to jog with me. Intentionally, I stayed a few steps ahead, but looked back every few seconds to check. But I had probably forgotten to check for some time, as all of a sudden, I heard stray dogs barking and growling. Turning back, I ran towards Ashish, shouting at the top of my voice; he also started running towards me as fast as he could.

Before I could reach and take control of the situation and disperse the dogs, the canine closest to Ashish bit him. He cried, more out of panic than pain. I took him to the hospital immediately; he had to take a few injections over the next month, and everything was fine soon enough. But he was frightened of stray dogs for several years after that incident.

When a father assumes the role of a coach, he faces a dilemma—how much of a push is too much? How can one instil the virtues of walking the extra mile, setting out on an adventure, or trying something new? Too big a push, and you risk leaving the child with a scar, maybe even a handicap. Too much mollycoddling, and the child is left with subpar growth and development. I reminded myself of the famous quote by John A. Shedd—'A ship in harbour is safe, but that is not what ships are built for'.

All along, Shilu was doing well in school. Influenced and encouraged by my commitment and interest, she had developed an early liking towards singing. I had always wanted to learn vocal music formally, and it is not a crime for parents to live vicariously through their children, so I enrolled her into a Hindustani classical lessons offered by the talented Mrs Nivedita Dutta. Shilu went on to complete Gandharva Mahavidyalaya exams for the prarambhik, praveshika pratham, and praveshika poorn levels in Hindustani classical music. She was also a voracious reader of storybooks of all kinds, such as age-appropriate comics and novels. Children benefit in many ways by interacting with their peers, and we were fortunate to have quite a few friends with children of similar age groups. We made a conscious effort to nurture these friendships and spend as much time with them as possible, so that both Shilu and Ashish could learn to make friends and develop enjoyable childhood memories with them.

Our children were lucky to be exposed to more than one parenting style. They benefitted immensely from the time spent with grandparents. Bou had been around Shilu a lot more than Ashish, who missed out on her company partly because we moved around quite a bit when he was a toddler, and Bou was unable to keep pace and accompany us. However, both our children had a special chemistry with my parents.

By far the most memorable time the six of us, spanning three generations, spent together were our travels to the four holy shrines together called Char Dham—Rameswaram, Dwarka, Badrinath and Puri. I remember our trek from Gaurikund to the Kedarnath temple; both my parents were carried in palkis (palanquins), seven-year-old Ashish was carried along in a basket on the back of a young man (locally called 'kandi'), while Shilu trekked the entire fifteen-kilometre uphill stretch with Bini and me. We reached the temple in the evening, and after offering prayers and witnessing the evening aarti, when we returned to our hotel, both Bou and Nana were quite shaken by the biting cold. 'What else do we plan to see here?' Nana asked, and seeing a blank look on my face, continued, 'Let us trek down as early as we can tomorrow morning.' I nodded.

At night, huddling between Bini and I, Ashish asked, 'Daddy, I am curious and want to ask you a question, but only if you promise you will not get angry.'

I promised.

'Did we have to trek this hard, all the way up in this bitter cold, just to see this small shrine?'

I did not have a reason to get angry, but I didn't want to evade his question either. 'This trek was important for Bapa and Maa. They always wanted to visit Char Dham along with you and Shilu. Their desire is now fulfilled. But look at it from a different angle—pilgrimage means different things to different people. While Bapa and Maa derived much pleasure as pilgrims, I am sure you and Shilu enjoyed the grandeur of the Himalayas and the beautiful state of Uttarakhand. We also visited the pretty towns of Rishikesh and Haridwar. Did you not enjoy crossing the Ganga on the Lakshman Jhula? And on our way back, we are going to spend time at the majestic confluences of the Ganga at Rudraprayag and Devprayag. Growing up, you will read about all these landmarks in your textbook, and cherish these memories. Now tell me, was the trip worth the effort or not?'

I could sense the seven-year-old tightening his grip around my neck. Huddling against me and warming my chest with his breath, he muttered, 'Thank you Daddy!'

Apart from spending significant time at work, since the discovery of his dyslexia, I had been with Ashish a lot, so my time with Shilu had been considerably reduced. Moreover, I had been noticing Shilu spending all her time indoors, reading books or rehearsing vocal music. I began to play badminton with her after returning from work every evening, so that I could accomplish my twin objectives of spending some quality time with her, and getting us both some exercise.

I used to jog for an hour every morning, after which I bowled around fifty deliveries to Ashish before taking a shower and driving to work. Adding badminton to the routine ended up straining my right shoulder. I ignored early warning signs, and after a while,

I tried to ease the strain by not playing the tabla, or table tennis, and so on. But that didn't help much. I stopped jogging, but still there was no relief. I stopped bowling and playing badminton, and consulted a doctor at Manipal Hospital. After looking at the x-ray, he banned any activity involving the right shoulder, and put me on pain killers. From a state of hyperactivity to a grinding halt in less than a week—it felt like imprisonment.

Midway through the first week of this inactivity, I suddenly paused one morning while brushing my teeth. 'This is an activity I can try with my left hand,' I thought, and switched hands. It felt awkward for a moment, no doubt, but soon I learnt to manoeuvre the toothbrush with the left hand. There was hope yet! The same morning, I bowled (or rather, threw) a few underarm deliveries at Ashish with my left hand. Curiosity grew.

In office, I tried playing table tennis using my left hand. I did not win any games, but created enough trouble for the opponents with left-handed forearm serves that made the ball bounce off the left-hand corner of the table for them. Right-handed players with weak backhands struggled to return the shot. I felt encouraged. In the evening, I played badminton with Shilu using my left hand.

The journey continued; I enjoyed concentrating on my left hand more than I had ever cared about my right. I would not quite claim to be ambidextrous, but by the time my right arm was back to normal, I had already learnt to use my left hand for most of my day-to-day chores.

Post this discovery, I began using my left hand for many activities as a conscious choice to rest the right. Gradually, certain activities involving both arms, like gardening, swimming and moving heavy things felt easier.

At times, we obsess and drive ourselves into a frenzy over a loss, temporary or permanent, instead of exploring the best possible use of what we already have. I would never have realized this piece of philosophy had I not engaged with the various facets of my children's upbringing.

Growing up, Shilu and Ashish had observed my devotion to Pranab Kishore Patnaik and Jagjit Singh—both of whom had one thing in common, that they put the divinity of music over their own personal popularity. The cassette and CD players at home and in the cars always played their songs, and I had also taken my children to a Jagjit Singh concert once. But my admiration for Pranab Kishore Patnaik was at a different level—unbeknownst to him, he was my guru, and one of my deepest desires was to pay guru dakshina to him.

The opportunity for that finally came in 2005, when Bangalore's Odisha Cultural Association planned to organize a musical night by a famous singer from the state, on the occasion of Ganesh puja. I not only proposed the name of Pranab Kishore Patnaik by pledging my commitment to sponsor the honorarium to be paid to him (this is something he does not know till date), but also ensured that I picked him up in my car from the train station, and hosted him and his troupe for a dinner and practice session at our home. The next evening, midway through his live concert, he took a pause, expressed his appreciation for the hospitality he received at our home, and invited me to sing a song. Singing one of his own songs—impromptu, without referring to lyrics—was the best way to pay tribute to my idol. When I dropped him off at the train station the next day, Pranab Kishore Patnaik had already become Pranab bhai to me.

We are the product of our own karma, no doubt. But we are also influenced and inspired by the invisible forces and personas around us, like Pranab bhai for me. We must look for ways to express our gratitude and pay tribute to them. Seeking blessings and goodwill make us humble and receptive to input and impetus. Not only did

I want to preach this to both my children, but I also wanted them to experience this first-hand by being a part of the festivity.

It is not that only parents influence their children; it could be the other way around too, and such influences can turn out to be the most enlightening ones.

This incident took place in 2006, during a visit to Karnataka's most famous historical site, Hampi. By the time we had been to the Virupaksha Temple and all other monuments at this UNESCO World Heritage Site, it was already evening. We rushed to the last stop on our list, the Tungabhadra Dam, but I missed out on my long-cherished wish of seeing the sun set over the dam. Nevertheless, we thought we would just swing by the site so that no box remained unchecked.

We reached there at around seven, and disappointed that it was too late to see anything or take pictures, were about to return. Ashish wanted a picture of the dam site with a statue of a lion in the background, and I had just clicked one, when a policeman rushed towards us, shouting 'no photography at the dam site'. He snatched the camera and asked me to follow him to the inspector. The entire set of pictures from the trip was in that camera, so I made to follow him, but our driver stepped in and started bargaining with the policeman.

'Sir, we have just clicked one picture without knowing the rules. Please consider,' he suggested, and the policeman looked like he was about to enter into a negotiation. But that's when both Shilu and Ashish intervened, saying, 'What? This sounds like a bribe! No Daddy, never do that. Let us go to the inspector and hold a conversation with him. If he listens to our plea, it will be great, else let him take the camera roll. We can take a few pictures of the monuments tomorrow morning. Even if we can't, we'll be fine without pictures!'

The policeman was stunned; his tough stand softened as he handed the camera back to me. The children thanked him while I stared dumbfoundedly at them, with a mix of awe and pride.

I like to believe that Bini and I had a role in inculcating many habits in them, consciously, over time. We always made sure that they woke up early and ate breakfast regularly. They never were given the option to say 'no' to fruits and eggs at breakfast, and vegetables and rotis at dinner. They were given the freedom to select what they wanted for lunch in their school canteens. That is the upside of giving reasonable freedom to children, you can then demand discipline when it really matters.

We had another best practice—except for the days when I was out on business travel, I used to make sure that I ate dinner at home, and we all ate together. Our dinner table indeed used to be the place where we caught up with each other's activities during the day. Reflecting on that, we derive immense pleasure and pride from the fact that we never ever discussed petty topics involving religion or caste.

I desired to see the growth of both of our children in multiple dimensions: physical, mental, emotional, spiritual and intellectual. Bini and I, therefore, discussed topics that could be openly discussed when our children were around; that way, we had little scope and time to engage in gossip. Education meant more than high scores on a report card.

Right or wrong, I had made a conscious effort not to push Shilu or Ashish to pay disproportionate attention to academics. I would glance at their report card after every exam and give input on subjects that fell below a reasonable threshold. Only during her tenth grade did I follow a different routine for Shilu—in the three months before her board exams, I would return home before six in the evening to make sure she was studying sincerely for at least four hours every evening. That discipline alone pushed her marks from around 80 per cent in the preparatory exams to beyond 90 per cent in the boards.

Shilu was probably unaware of the extent to which I was observing her work. While glancing over the chapter on 'the laws of indices' in maths, I challenged her once: 'Mama, I can bet you will not be able to solve question number eight.'

She was stunned by the pinpointed comment; to her, it almost felt like an intrusion. She took it as a challenge, and almost as if to prove me wrong, she started solving all the ten questions. To her utter disbelief, she could solve all but one—question number eight. With moist eyes, she asked me to solve that question.

'Daddy, how could you predict it so confidently?'

'When I was in my tenth grade, I also had most of these problems in our syllabus. I was unable to solve this particular question then, and I was challenging you to see if you could solve it,' I answered. To this day, Shilu chuckles while recalling this anecdote.

The real coaching session that evening did not end with solving question number eight together; it began there.

'If you had not solved all the ten questions, would you have realized you would not be able to solve question number eight?' I asked. 'Now imagine, if you had faced the same question in the exam, you would have been taken by surprise, isn't it?'

She nodded.

'The reward for solving as many questions as possible is not only to make you feel confident about what you know, but also to make you aware of what you do not know. In addition, it increases your speed of problem solving, thereby allowing you more time to attempt unfamiliar, difficult questions during the exam,' I said, and left my daughter with something to reflect upon that night.

The children were growing up and doing well. I had made it clear to both that it was their career; they would need to realize and work towards it. Unlike most Indian families, where parents push their children to pursue either an engineering or a medical degree, I wanted both my children to pursue things close to their heart. My only condition was that whatever they pursued, they had to be sincere about it. Shilu was genuinely passionate about biology and wanted to be a doctor, and I encouraged her all along. Ashish was still too young to decide what he wanted to do.

In the meantime, Whitefield had been transformed into a concrete jungle; the pace of development and the rate of inflow of MNCs into the area was beyond comprehension. Apart from being known as India's Silicon Valley, Bangalore was in the news for the wrong reason: traffic jams. Commuting woes had been draining significant mental energy, so I built a new house closer to work. I was enjoying the new home and driving around in a BMW 5 series sedan (thanks to my employer, GE), and planning to settle down in Bangalore long term.

As Woody Allen once said, 'If you want to make God laugh, tell him about your plans.' I was asked to pack my bags and travel to GE Energy Headquarters in Schenectady, New York, as the general manager of steam turbine engineering. It was another reminder; a scrapper should probably never make his own plans.

In hindsight, it was not a bad development. My role as the head of the India Engineering Centre for GE Infrastructure businesses had expanded; the team had gotten bigger, and so had my paycheque, but it was beginning to feel somewhat monotonous. Learning had reached a plateau. So, I started looking forward to the change and relocating to the United States.

During my last year in Bangalore, I probably should have paid more attention to Shilu, especially in her preparations for the competitive exams. Though her heart was set on becoming a paediatrician, she had not taken her medical entrance exams seriously. Eventually, she secured admission to biomedical engineering at the Manipal Institute of Technology. It was a difficult decision, both for Shilu and for us, but letting her pursue biomedical engineering seemed the best option at that juncture, so she stayed on in India while Bini, Ashish and I moved to the US.

In my new role in the US, leading the design and development of steam turbines tested my relearning and back-to-basics engineering skills. During my tenure, we attempted ambitious performance improvement, weight and span reduction programmes, and resolved several age-old steam turbine fleet issues. In January 2009, along with one of the vice-chairmen of GE, John Krenicki, I visited the three largest power equipment manufacturing companies in China—Shanghai Electric Group Company Limited, Hangzhou Steam Turbine Company Limited, and Harbin Electric Company Limited. It was quite an eye-opening experience. Subsequently, I travelled to Belfort (France), Warsaw (Poland), Florence (Italy) and Queretaro (Mexico).

Apart from work, each time I visited a country, I learnt a thing or two about its history, culture and business environment.

Career apart, I served as the co-chair of the Asia Pacific American Forum (APAF), one of the four affinity groups in GE that time. I carry memories of APAF members gathering in Schenectady Central Park for the annual park-cleaning event in spring, digging out loads of wet leaves buried under the snow for five months, collecting them in hundreds of biodegradable brown paper bags, hand-lifting and loading them in our personal car trunks to compost grounds, and enjoying coffee, donuts and pizza lunch at the end of the momentous undertaking. Thanks to APAF, Bini and I made great friends—Kapil and Nidhi, Ajai and Garima, Kamesh and Soujanya, Anil and Anjana, Mansi and Sujit, Ravi and Deepa, Kuiyang and Feifei, and Nafis and Akbar, to name a few.

My job was going great, and Ashish was also having a great run through middle school. Shilu's life, on the other hand, hit a roadblock.

If meeting the school principal had served as a wake-up call about Ashish, I did receive a real wake-up call about Shilu—the caller was Shilu herself.

'I am sorry, Daddy. I misused the freedom you granted me. I let you down. I did badly in my exams, abandoned my studies, and have fled from the Manipal campus,' she said, in tears.

I had confidence that she would confide in me, but for once, I felt I probably had granted her more freedom than I should have. She had enjoyed the freedom in the college hostel initially, but later felt lonely, lost focus and along with it, sight of her career.

There was no point in losing sleep over the past, nor was that the time to analyse. The best course of action was to act and make amends quickly.

'Where are you now? Are you safe, Mama?' I asked.

'I am in Goa, I have money, and I am absolutely safe, Daddy. Please do not worry about my safety,' she said, providing some relief to me.

'Wherever you are, return to our home in Bangalore first. You may have lost two years; it will not matter much in the long run. All along, you wanted to be a paediatrician, didn't you? May be that is God's plan. God has granted you another chance; we will put your dream back on track. Everything happens for a reason, Mama. I am arranging for your ticket; soon, you will board your flight to the US, and we will figure out the rest once you arrive here,' I assured her while trying to recover from the shock.

As intended, I had secured her provisional admission to Union College, Schenectady. Upon her arrival in the US, we formalized her admission as a biology major. She had learnt her lesson, so we continued to give her freedom, and allowed her to live in her college dorm, even though it was just a couple of miles away. She used to visit us—unprompted—on the weekends. That way, she spent more time where it was needed: with her friends and professors in college, and at the same time, she was not completely detached from us, especially from Ashish.

On Shilu's first day in Union College, I met her roommate Kara. Bini and I quite liked her demeanour. She hailed from New York City. With time, Shilu and she became close friends. She visited our home many times. Shilu also visited her luxurious apartment home in Manhatton. It was comforting to see both growing up together, sharing and caring, and learning from each other's cultural heritage.

We knew that we would want to live in the United States for the next several years, more so for the education of our children than my career. My assignment was also progressing well. My employer GE sponsored our permanent resident card (green card) in the EB-1 category, and we received our green cards promptly.

The following few years marked a different phase of the children's transformation. We travelled to many places together, as they progressed through their college and high school respectively. Shilu won many friends because of her singing talent, though she remained more focused on academics and prepared for the Medical College Admission Test (MCAT). Ashish consistently improved his standing in class while transitioning from his interest in cricket to football, and making many friends along the way. He exhibited immense interest and leadership in the state MathCounts and Science Bowl competitions, and represented his school in the Model UN confluence held in Philadelphia.

I wanted my children to realize that freedom is granted alongside responsibility. At the same time, I also wanted them to realize that I was always interested in their development, and to have the confidence that I was beside them when they really needed me. What makes children thrive is not protectionism and micromanagement, but granting more freedom and occasional supervision at critical checkpoints. The best way to make children run faster is to run behind them, and close in at times so that they try even harder. But never overtake them.

Life, at this point, seemed good in every way—financial stability, children on track with their careers, gorgeous summers and picturesque autumns (falls) of north-eastern USA, driving a BMW and a Porsche Cayenne, and owning a house. Moreover, Bini and I got involved in many social activities, some revolving around our own hobbies, and others in support of Shilu and Ashish's activities and interests. With inspiration from Manasi Dutta, a friend and colleague from GE, Bini and I got hooked on to long-distance running, and completed our first Mohawk Hudson River half-marathon. The run was held on a Sunday, 10 October 2010, and thus, the inscription '10/10/10' appeared on the jerseys, making it more memorable. We ran several half-marathons together, and influenced many more colleagues to run. Shilu and Ashish also joined us in running a half-marathon event. I even went on to complete my first full marathon a year later.

Yet, something was still not feeling right.

I had not relocated to the US to fulfil these desires. I was slipping into a comfort zone that was somehow making me feel an absence of purpose.

Deep in my heart, I always had and continue to have a special corner for my own country. I had been making meaningful contributions in a small way, in addressing issues that are prevalent in the country: helping employment, primary education, skill building and sanitation, to name a few. That is the reason I cherished my assignment at JFWTC Bangalore. I was missing that feeling while living in the United States. One primary reason that had enticed me to take up the steam turbine engineering leadership role was the hope that investment in India's power sector will accelerate exponentially, and that India will not only place orders for importing many steam turbines, but would also become home to many global steam turbines manufacturing companies, thereby creating large-scale infrastructure development and employment opportunities. Hedging my bets on this possibility I had also increased the strength and capabilities of the steam turbine engineering team in JFWTC Bangalore, exponentially, under the leadership of one of my trusted colleagues, Ajit Tulo. Business news was full of headlines about Tata Power's Mundra Ultra Mega Power Project (UMPP), and Larsen & Toubro forming a joint venture with Mitsubishi Heavy Industries to make steam turbines and generators for the power sector. The Mundra UMPP was, of course, commissioned to its full capacity by 2013, but the hype around coal-fired power plants providing an abundance of electric power to jumpstart India's economic development had died down.

As a company, GE had also undergone a sea change. It was not the same company that I was attracted to a decade ago. The leaders who were my role models all along had quit. I am someone who has always derived inspiration from the ecosystem around me, and it wasn't inspiring me anymore.

My forte had been to change the self, instead of blaming or tolerating the ecosystem. Instead of perspiring over things that were beyond my control, I thought of looking beyond GE, in a company with significant interest and presence in India.

The thought of starting my own business crossed my mind, but Shilu was just about to enter her medical programme and Ashish was in the final year of high school. I thought of continuing a salaried job, at least for some more time.

Indian youth needed jobs. Once one young individual joins the workforce, the entire family gets a boost. The individual may quit one company and join another; that's not a bad thing, because it paves the way for another aspiring young talent to gain employment. It was a mystery to me, and yet inspiring at the same time, that TCS was recruiting thousands of fresh talent from universities year after year, even when the business climate was facing significant headwinds.

I recalled my parting moment with Mr Ramadorai and Mr Chandrasekaran about a decade ago. I was in sporadic touch with both (never underestimate the value of New Year's and Diwali greetings!). The bridge to TCS could still be open for me, and with this belief in mind, I approached Mr Ramadorai, who in turn relayed my desire to Mr Chandrasekaran, who had become the CEO and MD of TCS by then.

Mr Chandrasekaran offered me the role of global head of learning and development (L&D) at TCS. Habitually, I do not worry about the nature of my role, but I was somewhat worried this time, as the role that was offered to me was neither something that had anything to do with my educational qualifications, nor did it have much relevance to my twenty-five years of professional experience. But Mr Chandrasekaran is among the most powerful influencers I have ever come across in my career. 'At the moment, finding a leader to take up the role of L&D head is an organizational need,' was the one line through which he enticed me to the role.

I also contemplated that this role would have the purpose, potential and the ability to influence the careers of thousands of young talents, which I was longing for. I accepted the role and moved to TCS Thiruvananthapuram (Kerala) in June 2013. I went alone, leaving behind Bini in the US to oversee Ashish's final high school year and Shilu's pre-med programme.

10

REDISCOVERING THE SELF

The events of 6 December 2013 resonate vividly in my memory. It was a Friday, and after the regular business hours, I set out for my evening jog with one of my colleagues. We routinely covered a five-kilometre track around our learning centre in Thiruvananthapuram, but somehow, it seemed particularly challenging that day. I ignored the discomfort, completed the run, and later did a few stretches and abdominal exercises. Returning to the company guest house, I took a shower and nestled against the couch, sipping a cup of tea. To my disbelief, the usually refreshing drink failed to pull me together that evening. I recall that I had sipped around ten cups of tea and coffee during office hours that day, and felt queasy. I threw up, and the concerned caretaker offered help, but ignoring him, I skipped dinner that night and laid down to sleep. The discomfort continued, but I assured myself that it would soon pass.

I was in better spirits the next morning. As it was a weekend, I decided to relax, drink sufficient fluids and stick to a light diet.

It was on Monday that I met my doctor, on the way to the office. He advised an ECG, and I met him again with the report the following day. Noticing a slight irregularity in the pattern, he advised me to see a cardiologist. It was already the fifth day after that restless 6 December evening, and five days of 'negligence' or 'madness' ended when I met Colonel Nair, a father figure from the TCS Thiruvananthapuram administration team. With his influence, I managed to get an appointment with the Padma Shri-awardee cardiologist Dr G. Vijayaraghavan of KIMS Hospital. I met him with another set of blood tests and ECG reports, and after examining me and going through them, he confirmed it had been a heart attack!

I was immediately admitted to the ICU, and was discharged only after a week of treatment. A few weeks of regulated lifestyle later, I went back to work. I would like to share with you five learnings from this event that had caught me unawares.

1. Physical and mental fatigue had crept in due to the hectic schedule of the preceding weeks. I chose to engage in physical activities to clear my head, but my body was unprepared. I didn't pay heed to the pangs of discomfort experienced during exercise, which was a big mistake. I convinced myself that the discomfort could be of a gastric nature. I thought I was absolutely fit, and a heart attack was out of the question. Overconfidence, bordering on arrogance, almost proved too costly. *Your body is your closest friend, listen to it.*

2. Within the first few minutes of getting admitted to the ICU, I realized I had had a close shave. Though I functioned normally, I was on the verge of collapse during those five days. I surrendered myself completely to the expert care of

the medical team at the hospital. My colleagues turned up en masse at the hospital. When I was being taken to the operation theatre, I could see all of them lined up, with disbelief and shock written on their faces. Their eyes shone with concern, radiating the prayers running through their minds. Their presence tided over the absence of my family at that crucial moment. *Your world is much bigger than you think.*

3. I did not understand the course of events in the operation theatre. The only thing I knew for sure was that the doctors would continue the treatment, and take another angiogram the next day. It was evening, and I realized my iPhone had been taken away. I had nothing to do. I suddenly felt conscious of the free time I never had before. I was perfectly in my senses and wanted to talk to people around me. I addressed the staff nurses by name, and they loved it. Every opportunity Syiji got, she talked about her seven-month-old daughter. Aswathi tried to impress me with her Hindi vocabulary. Saju discovered a captive listener in me, and spent long hours preaching his philosophy. When it was close to midnight, everyone advised me to close my eyes and get some sleep, in vain. I started humming my favourite old ghazals. I felt a sense of thrill in recalling the lyrics of those melodies that I had never sung for decades, and which were beginning to fade away. So there I was, experiencing a dollop of serenity in an ICU. What would I have gained by worrying about the things that were not in my control? *There is beauty in losing control and surrendering yourself completely to the moment.*

4. It is up to us to learn from the past, be diligent in the present, and reset our future. After being discharged from

the hospital, I decided to reinvent my ecosystem. I learnt how to prepare a completely healthy yet tasty meal without using a single drop of oil; how to enjoy black and green tea without sugar or sweeteners. I have been walking a couple of hours regularly, and hopefully, I will be able to resume my favourite long-distance running sometime soon. But I will never ignore the feedback from my own body. *Every adverse situation can do one of two things to you—shake you up and derail you, or bring meaningful realignment to your life.*

5.   I have been a runner and fitness freak throughout my life. I consistently maintain the ideal blood pressure, and am not diabetic. I don't sweat over small things. I do have a bit of cholesterol, but that alone should not be a reason to trigger a heart attack. My family, relatives and friends have been asking why it occurred. My doctor had no answer to the question either. I have realized *not to overanalyse things and instead, take life as it comes!* Life is, after all, a journey, not a destination. It is a continuous function till a point of discontinuity precipitously appears somewhere along the journey. And whenever that point of discontinuity appears, I hope, I will have a moment to pause, smile, wish good luck to my fellow passengers, and whisper to myself—what a ride it was!

THE ABOVE IS NOT A fictional account—it is a slightly edited version of the first-ever blog post I wrote on 'KNOME', an internal social media platform in TCS.

In high school, I received a wake-up call from Pandit sir, and in response, I took Sanskrit seriously. As a parent in Bangalore, I received a wake-up call from the principal Mrs Hemchandani, and in response, I took my son's dyslexia seriously and kept working with him until he was fine. As a parent in the US, I received a wake-up call from my daughter, and in response, I intervened, influenced, and oversaw the course-correction in her career and life.

Whenever life threw curve-balls at me, I never ducked them, but received them as wake-up calls. The heart attack, though, was rather hard, and had a different impact on me. I learnt to listen to my body. I had to resort to several course corrections in my lifestyle: I stopped making long-term plans, and instead, learnt to live life in smaller increments—a day, a month, or at most, a year at a time.

I had been granted an extension to my life, and I accepted this gift with humility and moved on. Unbelievably, after enduring this, I became somewhat fearless. Many treat such issues as personal and prefer to keep them private; I opted to make it public instead. The price I paid for my negligence, and the learning I received the hard way, must be passed on for the benefit of others, I thought. In fact, though the blog post appeared three weeks after my hospital stint, I had conceptualized it while I was recovering in the ICU itself.

The blog post went viral, and within a couple of days, received more than seven thousand views, close to a thousand likes and comments, and got shared over a hundred times in several communities.

Encouraged, I posted a few more blog entries on diverse topics. Most of them received wide readership. I discovered something I never thought had lived in me all along: the skill of writing.

I was not on Facebook then, nor was I very active on LinkedIn. But I got hooked to KNOME. Being an internal platform, I could share intimate real-life stories there. At some point, I shared how my father had disciplined and imbibed in me the habit of not wasting food. Through another blog post, I shared how I was punished by my father for stealing and using a soap that never belonged to us, thus impressing in my mind that we should not take what we cannot afford.

My writings and interactions particularly engaged the younger generation. I wanted them to realize that they had no reasons to make excuses. Coming from a humble background, if I could evolve with time and do reasonably well in my career, all of them could. I wanted them to derive confidence from my life story, believe in themselves, and never stop evolving.

In retrospect, I believe that the role of the chief learning officer of TCS stretched my abilities the most, by far. In most of the roles I had stepped into earlier in my career, I had the knowledge and experience to hit the ground running. But this role was different; I was not an HR professional. To make a meaningful contribution to the role, I had to learn the art and science of learning, and imbibe the fundamental attributes of learning professionals. That required spending significant amounts of time going downstream, learning not only from my direct reports or the L&D leaders, but also from their teams. A curious mind that is willing to learn and generate new ideas can ask good questions, especially while challenging the status quo. That is exactly what happened. Face-time with the team was inspiration for them, and for me, it was the best time I had spent, learning something refreshing and different from ground up.

Even though I had little knowhow of the job, I always had a great team behind me, like I did at the EACoE and BEC and JFWTC. The difference, however, was that I had handpicked the leaders on those teams, whereas in TCS, I had inherited an already existing L&D leadership team. Of course, I made a few changes, and effected them rather quickly. But the core team remained nearly the same. What was needed was to trust their abilities, and back them.

First things first, I had chosen Thiruvananthapuram as my work location, since it was viewed as the Mecca of learning and development in TCS. The first dedicated campus for TCS's ILP was built in the Technopark there. However, my immediate predecessors didn't work out of the capital of Kerala, so the campus had lost its lustre. The land where the campus was built was low-lying; there was a huge issue of waterlogging in the monsoons. The ILP hostel inside the campus was shut down, as the sewage treatment plant was non-functional. The state of affairs called for large-scale re-engineering efforts, and I was instrumental in hiring a professional, Subair P.H., specializing in facilities maintenance. When it was all done, the campus looked truly vivacious, especially when the ILP hostel returned to its normal operations, and the programme ran to its full capacity.

One of my early observations was that there were too many 'early and mid-career' leadership development programmes in TCS, with little organic linkage between them. None of them was attended by a critical mass of prospective leaders; hence they lacked intensity and impact. More worrisome was the fact that most of those programmes were external, run by mom-and-pop-shop personalities. I gathered the courage to sunset most of them, and inspired Dr Sharada Ganesh and her leadership development team—Smitha Balakrishnan, Suraj Ramakrishnan and Usha Bharathi—to create early and mid-career leadership development programmes in-house. The first-line leadership programme 'ASCENT' was the first of several in this evolution. I liked the name ASCENT, so I asked the team to come up with a meaningful list of attributes that could exemplify this acronym. They creatively came up with this:

A: Augmenting Capabilities—The Opening Strides

S: Succeeding with Stakeholders—Concur to Conquer

C: Collaborating for Results—Buy-in for Success

E: Enabling Managerial Acumen—The Soul of Project Management

N: Nourishing the Leader Within—Realize Your Potential

T: Teaming Up—Transform to Perform

ASCENT is just one example; it was unbelievable that whatever idea I threw at the leaders in the L&D team, they took it seriously. Conventional leaders formulate their strategy surreptitiously in boardrooms; I formulated TCS's L&D strategy by bouncing my thoughts off my own team. Continuing the best practices gained from my experience in previous organizations, I held quarterly virtual townhall meetings to recognize and inspire exceptional team performances, and share short-term and long-term organizational perspectives. Long-term for me did not really mean anything more than a year. That truly worked in driving accountability, realizing progress and making early course-corrections if needed.

While travelling to major TCS locations, I learnt that each was following an isolated regional learning calendar, and had its own uncoupled learning infrastructure. Learning as a talent-enabling phenomenon was simply not scalable. That is when the thought of the 'Global Learning Calendar' originated. Such a learning calendar cannot be easily deployed in an instructor-led training environment. 'Digital learning' as a phenomenon was also in a state of infancy in the industry, and I believed TCS could be the trendsetter in leveraging technology to enable a virtually augmented training ecosystem. At scale, globally.

To bring out radical changes in a CXO-level role, unequivocal support of the leadership is crucial. I had the encouragement and support of the TCS leadership, especially my boss, Mr Ajoy Mukherjee, to experiment and implement large-scale changes to the learning platform, programmes and pedagogy. That helped in sunsetting the age-old external learning management system (LMS) adopted by TCS thus far, and replacing them with one built indigenously. Connecting learning as the pathway to evolution, the new LMS was named iEvolve. The integration of iEvolve with TCS iON, the state-of-the art content consumption and assessment platform, created a formidable learning ecosystem that stood the test of time.

Discharging the responsibility at a CXO level calls for chasing audacious goals. 'Let us upskill a hundred thousand employees in digital skills in one fiscal year,' Mr Chandrasekaran challenged, though it took some time to come to fruition.

During the fiscal year 2015-16, the audacious goal was followed through relentlessly and realized anyway. The regional L&D heads under the leadership of Debtanu Paul, especially Swarnasudha Selvaraj and Dharshana Karthik from Chennai, Praveen Ashok from Bengaluru (as it was called now), programme creation and organization by Anupama Raghavendra and Nidharshana Narayanan, and programme management by Rajkishore Jha and Veena Purohit played pivotal roles in this journey.

Often, isolated self-learning ends up being ineffective due to lack of guidance, interactions and mental simulation. The significance of a 'guru' has been established since time immemorial—a guru not only tells you what to learn, but also influences how to learn, and most importantly, why to learn. The immersive learning experience in the company of peers with a guru in a gurukul cannot be replicated.

How would an organization as large and diverse as TCS set up its gurukuls? Where, and how many? How would a digital-age Dronacharya manage these gurukuls? The introspection of these questions stimulated the idea of virtual gurukuls in my mind.

The concept of a virtual gurukul is not something new. It was exemplified by Ekalavya, who set up his own virtual gurukul and learnt archery independent of place and time. All he needed was the inspiration of his virtual guru—an idol, not the guru himself. That is the best example and precursor to 'anytime, anywhere' modern-age learning.

Every learner, however, is not as self-inspired as Ekalavya. A conventional learner needs to be guided by a subject matter expert, either from his or her workplace or in a live classroom. Someone who can curate useful courses out of the plethora of online learning content, set up periodic assessments and sample questions to help learners do self-checks, and ensure application through stimulating discussions, engaging learners through activities and use of cases. That is precisely what happens through the TCS' iQlass network[1], which enables high-tech human touch in lieu of high-touch human touch. TCS, as an organization, is proud of this, and rightly so. I derive immense self-satisfaction and pride for providing the impetus behind the iQlass network worldwide.

Anytime, anywhere learning had become a buzz word in the industry, but it was still not adequate to deliver the speed, scale and spread of learning in as large and as diverse an organization as TCS. Unconventional goals cannot be accomplished by conventional means. If 'anytime' and 'anywhere' expanded the time and place horizons respectively, I made an indefatigable attempt to expand the coverage (anyone), streaming (any device) and source (any content) of learning ecosystem which, over time, matured to manifest in the form of the five As of learning[2].

Combining the digital learning platform, iQlass and the 5A framework, a state-of-the-art learning ecosystem was put in place.

You can lead a horse to water, but you can't make him drink—so the biggest issue was to create a learning culture in the organization. For that, what works better, the carrot or the stick? The stick is hard on people, and if not applied mindfully, the receiver can become resistant. The carrot costs money and can be addictive, setting unreasonable and unsustainable expectations in the long run.

Most students learn because they have to face exams. For some, an exam acts as a compelling need, while for others, it can also act as an enabler. The behaviour at a workplace is very different; there, learning is not a compelling need, especially for someone who is content.

We are in a state of permanent 'beta', and one must have the humility to accept this truth for evolution of the self.

For me, the path that appeared worth pursuing to create a learning culture in the organization was the path of enablement.

In an organization, especially, learning cannot be an end unto itself. To successfully create a vibrant learning culture, one would have to draw a direct line between learning and organizational goals. How was I to achieve that?

TCS's brand promise at the time was 'experience certainty'. I took a view of this declarative tagline and tried to see it through the lense of the talent ecosystem. The first thing that did not gel in my mind was the tagline of L&D function at the time, 'co-creating capabilities'. After giving some thought, I conceived two important changes to the talent ecosystem within TCS. First, the conventional L&D function was renamed and rebranded to a more contemporary name: talent development. Second, the passive tagline of the talent development function, co-creating capabilities, was changed to an active one: 'enabling certainty'. The promise of the talent development function to the broader TCS and its customers was enabling delivery certainty through the certainty of the talent ecosystem.

Such thought processes galvanized the members of the talent development function; motivation shot up. The team associated itself with the broader purpose.

My social media proclivity on KNOME suited my role. Social media could be a powerful medium, if used prudently. As the CLO of TCS, I took the plunge and used KNOME as a platform to influence and promote learning and sharing. Influencing without exercising authority is not an easy thing. I learnt and nurtured an important leadership attribute in this role.

Early on, through one of my blog posts, I had shared the famous Panchatantra story that characterizes two parrots growing up in contrasting environments: one at a butcher's house, revealing its fury at seeing a visitor, saying, 'a new prey has just arrived, kill him and chop off his head!'; the other at a priest's home, greeting the same visitor with, 'a new guest has just arrived, show him the guest room and offer him a glass of water'. With the story as the backdrop, I had coined the thought: 'Physically, we are what we eat; intellectually, we are what we learn.'

As I began to influence the readers, I realized the power of storytelling. When the stories were based on real-life experiences, they resonated well. 'The right time to pluck any vegetable is when you feel that it has stopped growing,' Bou's words rang in my mind, and I related them to career progression. As long as one continues to learn and grow, everyone is happy. Once learning stops, contribution reaches a plateau. Everyone around loses excitement, and the option left for an individual then is either to change or be content with a stagnating career. Connecting the significance of growing in one's career to the anecdote from my childhood was never perceived as preaching, but as experiential learning through real-life experience sharing.

Cajoling certainly engaged the learners. But for learning to be sustainable, the programmes had to be enticing, and their content engaging.

'Where should we spend most of our time—in building content or building the container?' I once asked members of the content development team. As expected, the opinion was divided.

I weighed in with my personal view. 'The look and feel of the container, or in other words, the packaging of the learning programmes, is important to create a good first impression and to entice the learners to engage. But once they enrol, the quality of the content will decide whether the programme creates a lasting impression or will soon be forgotten.'

I also believed in the voice of the participants, and so, reinforced: 'Never underestimate the power of the word of mouth. You want the programme participants to be your brand ambassadors. If they are happy with the programme content, they will also lure their colleagues to attend the programme.'

The team got the message. For the following few years, the TD team made it a priority to build and curate the most enriching and engaging content as the backbone of every in-house talent development programme.

There was a widespread perception that the newer generation has a shorter attention span. Personally, I feel it is a myth. A monotonous course will not be able to hold attention for long, irrespective of the learner's year of birth. 'The engagement could be better if content can be made modular. Retention of learning content and comprehension could be sustained if some sort of practice, in the form of interactive quizzes, can be introduced, at the end of every learning module,' I insisted. This thought gelled with the team. That was the beginning of the in-house production of a series of state-of-the-art 'nano learning videos' in TCS, using which, innumerable internal certification programmes were curated. The learning technology and learning content specialists—Krishna Murthy Awaar, Bidisha Sinha Roy and Sarulatha Dayalan, under the leadership of Laxmi Nair, Swarnasudha Selvaraj and Karthik S.—played a momentous role in this audacious journey.

We have heard the popular saying, 'walk the talk'. What about its opposite, 'talking the walk'? This question had amused me once. If 'walking the talk' meant putting one's words into action, 'talking the walk' would mean articulating one's action in words. For professionals in consulting and services-based organizations, it does not hurt to beat your own drum a bit. In my view 'articulation' is a unique and essential skill for white-collar professionals. Convincing the leadership or customers to get their proposed solutions accepted and funded is also part of their job. In fact, many professionals stumble right at this step.

Talking of articulation, I once listened to the then-CEO of TCS, Rajesh Gopinathan, addressing a batch of participants undergoing a sales leadership programme. His concept of three As—Awareness, Articulation and Amplification—intrigued me. As such, articulation as a learning programme had been tickling my mind for quite some time, and I was just looking for the right recipe. Taking a cue from Rajesh's three As, I inspired Dolon Gupta, the leader of the culture and language initiatives team in TCS, to build, pilot and launch a programme on articulation. The ensuing internal certification programme, 'Art of Articulation', engaged virtually every TCS employee in upskilling their storytelling and selling skills.

The TCS leadership had taken the plunge to build a 100 per cent 'agile workforce' by 2020. The first step in the journey was to train the entire workforce in a basic course, titled the 'agile way of working', and subsequently upskilling them to be agile practitioners. The talent development function had a pivotal role to play in this audacious journey.

To make a child walk, the parents also need to walk. Likewise, to make the employees learn, their leaders also need to learn.

I was among the first few to complete the 'agile way of working' course, and I didn't stop there. After walking the talk, I did a bit of talking the walk as well—I had scored 97 per cent marks in the course assessment, so through a blog post on KNOME, I not only flashed my personal score, but also inspired my TCS colleagues to take up the course and the assessment seriously, and if they pass, to flash their personal score as 'comments' to my post. I had promised to get in touch with the first ten respondents and have a special lunch meeting with the respondent who scored 100 per cent first.

That was the germination of a competitive peer-learning environment in TCS—social learning on a social platform at its best.

Inspiration helped engage quite a few employees in the learning process. 'Are you learning? If not, watch out, you may stop growing!' Some employees woke up to periodic nudges like this on KNOME. A vast majority of employees, however, are silent learners. All they needed was awareness and accessibility to learning programmes, and occasional handholding, so that they could learn at their own leisure. The 'inclusive learning pyramid' at TCS provided them the perfect answer.

I was always fascinated by the extravaganza called Dahi Handi. As a child, witnessing youngsters build magnificent human pyramids to crack open the jackpot of sweets on the day of Krishna Janmashtami every year simply used to take my breath away. I realized an organization is also a human pyramid; so, taking a cue from Dahi Handi, I conceptualized a one-page visual that provided a catalogued view of learning programmes and their linkage to career ambitions. This visual—the inclusive learning pyramid, later copyrighted as a TCS intellectual property—was so pervasive in the organization that if one walked into any major TCS office, one could find it displayed, especially on the walls of learning labs, iQlass network and auditoriums.

Between 2013 and 2019, when I worked as the CLO, TCS had, on average, been recruiting over 30,000 freshers from Indian universities every year. Inducting those free-spirited campus talents and metamorphosing them to world-class, responsible IT talents through the three-month residential TCS ILP had been a mammoth undertaking. Considering the sheer size, any tweak to the ILP had to be conceived, piloted and implemented diligently. A small mistake could have major consequences, and at the same time, a small improvement could generate recurring business value. Recognizing the online proclivity of students, we piloted the inclusion of a major portion of the ILP content into the final semester curriculum in a few colleges. The successful graduates from these colleges needed to go through a curtailed one-month residential ILP curriculum, thereby accelerating their integration into projects, with substantial training cost savings to TCS. Little did I know that this initiative, which I had nicknamed TCS Xplore, would later democratize the ILP and become a national phenomenon. Over a period of five years, seven of my colleagues—Suresh Panampilly, Gino Premila, S. Janardhan, Prathap Kolla, Annie Felix, VS Viju and Saji Joseph—and their teams played a commendable role in the TCS ILP reimagination journey.

Talent development as an intent and business-enabling function had gained unprecedented momentum within TCS. The five As of learning, conceptualization and institutionalization of the 'global learning calendar' and the 'inclusive learning pyramid' galvanized the learning culture within. The metamorphosis of a learning organization with hundreds of thousands of employees is difficult to comprehend internally; it is easier to reflect on the organization from the eyes of the external world. The L&D team of TCS was recognized as the 'best learning team' and 'global L&D team of the year' by Brandon Hall Group, and the Learning and Performance Institute, UK. Thanks to L&D's contribution to TCS as an organization, I was personally recognized as the 'global chief learning officer of the year' at the Tata Institute of Social Science's LEAPVAULT CLO summit in 2015; the best CLO of the year 2017 by the international *Chief Learning Officer* magazine[3]; and the 2018 Stevie award for great employers' CLO of the year. In 2018, TCS was one among three recognized as the best learning organizations globally by the Association of Talent Development (ATD), and in 2019, was honoured with the BML Munjal Award for sustained 'business excellence through learning and development'. It was a matter of pride for me personally to receive the coveted award from the chairman of BML Munjal group, Sunil Kant Munjal, and Pranab Mukherjee, Bharat Ratna awardee and former President of India.

Nivedita Kuruvilla, the leader of the communication and branding team, was the one who used to work with the talent development programme leaders to write the applications for various awards. I knew a few of those leaders, especially Nivedita, used to offer prayers for me to win the CLO of the year award.

I had followed the practice of convening all the leaders in TCS talent development team at the Leadership Development Institute (LDI) Trivandrum. This annual confluence was named as EnLighten. Two of my colleagues from TCS Thiruvananthapuram, R Deepthi and Praveena Pramod, had been putting in untiring efforts to organize this annual event year after year. One particular year, after the business discussions, while we were unwinding over an evening social event, I overheard a conversation among some of the leaders—'Our talent development function in TCS runs as a joint family.'

When the world outside validates and recognizes achievements, it certainly feels good. But the feeling we shared for each other within the talent development team was an even bigger achievement. The kinship was heartening. I moved on to a different role, but the leaders of the TCS talent development function continue to congregate and share camaraderie through EnLighten.

Over an informal farewell function, the team presented me with a gift, one of the most precious I have received in my career. It is a fridge magnet on which, apart from my picture, there is the inscription: 'Thank you—the leader who made us evolve; the challenges, the fun, the hard work, the achievements, the guidance, the motivation, the inspiration; thank you for the path and the journey!'

Before accepting the role of the CLO of TCS, I had no knowledge of the science and art of talent development. I learnt the nuances from the team. They might feel I made them evolve; the truth is, I evolved more than they did.

Accolades and awards will fade away in time, but the camaraderie with the team in the talent development reimagination journey will never ever be erased from my memory.

11

LIFE IN AN EMPTY NEST

WHETHER AT WORK OR AWAY from it, life is about getting the most value out of the currency called time. Even accounting for six to seven hours of sleep and a few hours for daily chores, most working professionals get five to seven hours of time to do something that matters to them—be it with family and friends, or by themselves. Doing something of personal interest in pursuit of happiness and meaning is important.

At the time of my hospitalization in December 2013, Bini was still in the US with Shilu and Ashish. I was in a state of self-denial; for a few months prior, I had been struck by the empty nest syndrome. During the recovery period, I had promised myself I would rebound meaningfully; that an empty nest could trigger something good too.

Not just at work, life also evolved on the personal front. I found solace in my new hobby, writing. It became my new passion.

I practiced not feeling lonely when I was indeed lonely, and it was possible.

As I resorted to serious writing, my interest in reading was renewed. It not only recharged my vocabulary, but also made me reflect. My reading became purposeful and my comprehension sharper. It expanded my thoughts organically and laterally. Some of my writings became extensions of thoughts triggered by reading. I realized what I had been missing all along: deep reading. I had not been taking the next logical steps—reflecting, drawing inferences, developing a personal point of view and writing. Not writing about the book, but on parallel and lateral topics.

I also started approaching my one-on-one discussions differently. I began to notice and recognize unique attributes in individuals, and often acknowledged them publicly in the form of inspiring stories, winning many hearts without actively seeking to. I never thought that the business lingo called the 'low hanging fruits' could apply to themes beyond business and material gains. I saw my influence on people around me grow with time, at no extra cost to me.

The comments on my blog posts made me realize another thing—readers were passionate about topics and had opinions, but often fell short when it came to articulation. Coming from a rural background, I could empathize. Stating a point of view at the right time is important in a career, else one runs the risk of just standing and watching as opportunities pass by. I thought of stirring up my established network of followers by posting on topics that could have very contrasting points of view, thereby engaging the readers, promoting sharing and learning among them. 'Would you prefer to do what you love, or love what you do?' was one of the early posts in this vein.

I started posting a unique topic every Monday morning at nine. This continued for three and a half years, totalling up to over 200 posts, hashtagged with #MondayMorningTrivia and #MMT. They became quite popular and stimulated informal learning. I would often present dilemmas that pushed my colleagues in TCS to think, develop a personal point of view, post comments, discuss opposing views, agree, disagree, like and influence each other's thinking.

More than the readers, the habit had an incredible impact on me personally. It improved my cognitive ability. I realized that what was playing out every Monday morning had its roots in something more profound. In the journey of life, we frequently come across forks in the road. We know that these paths lead in opposite directions, and each will result in life-changing consequences. And yet, we are faced with a series of such choices in life. I would build on the situations I faced or read about, and make the posts as intriguing and stimulating as possible. It also worked as a forcing function to my commitment. I would build a repository of possible topics as the week progressed. Come Sunday afternoon, I would pick one topic from the repository and spend a couple of hours developing the context and the content. I wanted to ensure that the context was compelling, the title enticing, and the content engaging enough to capture the attention of the highly skilled and talented colleagues of TCS.

Emojis can lie, but eyes cannot. I had therefore made it a practice to have one-on-one discussions with each and every member of the talent development team, which necessitated me to travel to each major TCS location in India and abroad.

The company has a big, beautiful office at Kalinga Park in Bhubaneswar. As a result, I found myself visiting my state's capital a bit more frequently than I used to, over the past several years. While in Bhubaneswar, I would commute from my village home instead of staying in hotels.

At my behest, my younger brother Shyama had built a beautiful farmhouse in our village. Frequent travel to Bhubaneswar not only ensured more face time with parents and siblings, but also meant a stronger reconnect with my village. Swimming in the pond, catching fish, growing and plucking vegetables in the farmland took me back in time. Our joint family over the last two decades had grown around me financially. The time now was ripe for us to spend more time together, sharing and caring. The vibe in the family brought bliss to my parents. Nana always wanted to help people, but he did not have the money. Seeing our financial well-being, he also opened his arms to the needy in our village.

The vibe in Kerala, especially inside TCS Thiruvananthapuram, reaches its peak during the Onam festival. Employees turn up in ethnic wear. In my first year on campus, during Onam, I noticed that the security and housekeeping staff were in their uniforms, which I felt was odd. 'They too need to be a part of the festivity. Let us ask them to dress in their ethnic wear as well,' I advocated. My proposal was met with stiff resistance. 'How would they perform their duties in ethnic wear?' But I was in no mood to step back without a convincing reason, and argued, 'if employees can perform their duties in ethnic wear, why can't the support staff?' Eventually, my proposal was accepted, and it was heartening to see the smiling faces of the support staff in their ethnic wear, enjoying the festive meal sadya.

Over in the US, Shilu's dream of becoming a paediatric doctor was a step closer as she joined the New York Medical College. Ashish, meanwhile, pursued his interest in finance at the University of California, Los Angeles (UCLA) as an economics major.

Our dreams for our children were coming true. After both moved to their colleges, Bini joined me in Thiruvananthapuram.

We bought a house in a newly developed gated community. I was accustomed to living alone and had succeeded in defying the empty nest syndrome. But Bini was living without Shilu and

Ashish for the first time. It was hard on her initially, but soon she also discovered her passion—she took up painting. We decided to influence Prasant, our caretaker from the Bangalore days, to come live with us, and he expanded his skills to become our driver, cook, and gardener, and an integral part of our family.

Our plot of land in Thiruvananthapuram came with a single neem tree and two coconut trees. The rest was covered in weeds, so we decided to do some gardening. I began by planting a few papaya, banana, mango, pomegranate and sapota (chikoo) plants. Seeing my commitment, Prasant tagged along and started a kitchen garden in the backyard. Bini made no personal contribution to the garden, but at her behest, Prasant planted a few flowering plants in the front garden. Soon, the house looked like a beautiful home, at least from the outside.

The morning walk through the hilly roads was absolute bliss; they pierced through tapioca, coconut and banana groves. Choosing to live in a suburb instead of the heart of the city meant less traffic and less pollution. Bini could speak a bit of Malayalam; we made many friends during our walks. Soon, walking outdoors became an essential part of our lifestyle, and since then, I have said goodbye to walking on treadmills.

One Sunday morning, I decided to relive the days before we had washing machines. I soaked a bucketful of clothes in liquid detergent and hand-washed them. The hot and sunny weather served as impetus, and I was fully absorbed, scrubbing the sweaty areas around the shirt collars and spots from spilt curry. Washing was fun; I never looked back at the washing machine again. If Sunday evenings were reserved for writing posts, mornings were well-utilized for washing clothes. Bini was happy, because the time and effort needed to operate the washing machine was cut in half. To me, the most important benefit came as a side effect—I got the much-needed exercise for my shoulder, elbow, knee, and hip joints.

Ironically, as a senior executive at TCS, I had been advocating automation at work, raising the performance bar for humans, while empowering machines to take over repetitive and uninspiring human tasks. The perception at the workplace was that machines were snatching jobs away from humans. At home, things were different; I was reclaiming jobs from machines. Repetitive and mundane tasks indeed felt rejuvenating.

I thought of extending the fitness routine to my workplace as well by resuming table tennis in the afternoons, and fortunately, discovered two enthusiasts in K. Kesavasamy and Suresh Panampilly. Suresh was good as a player, but Dr Samy, though the oldest among us, was the most competitive. It was quite a sight to see both playing each other—they would fight and tease each other like kindergarteners! We continued to play regularly for more than five years. Dr Samy's wife, Maithilly ma'am, still credits me for getting him back on his exercise routine. He himself had a different reason to rejoice—as a result of playing regularly, he had reduced his waistline by a couple of inches and was able to reclaim a dozen of abandoned pants from his wardrobe.

The quest for rewinding time and reviving as many forgotten hobbies and habits as possible was never ending. When I moved from village to college, I had to abandon the habit of using the traditional twig used to clean teeth—datun—and switch to a toothbrush instead, because there was no place to dispose of used datuns. The delights of datun were never ending, because it offered greater flexibility for customization than a toothbrush. Moderate chewing gave the feeling of an extra hard toothbrush; chewing some more would convert it to a medium-stiff brush; chewing even more would be as comfortable as an extra soft toothbrush. Splitting the twig longitudinally and using the split halves as tongue cleaners was absolutely refreshing. Bamboo and guava datuns were options, but neem was my personal favourite, especially because it brought back that moment with my siblings standing in the courtyard, looking up at the sky and performing the long and disgusting gargle, out aloud, until the bitterness of neem left our taste buds. Once that was gone, the rest of the day felt invigorating.

I yearned to relive those moments. I turned my gaze to the neem trees in our yard—the lone tree from a year ago had company now, in the form of several young trees and branches that it had given birth to. I thought it was the perfect opportunity for pruning, but not all at once. One branch at a time would make five to eight datuns, good enough for a week. Brushing with datuns is an environment-friendly act; the discarded branches and leaves are biodegradable. Moreover, honestly, since I started using neem datun, my love and care for the neem trees also went up. The not-so-good feeling of reusing the same toothbrush for several months, wasting precious running water, and ingesting chemicals in the form of toothpaste became things of the past.

Growing older, it was prudent to switch to healthier food habits. I have nothing against crisp masala dosa, soft idlis or parathas. It's not just the carb overload and cooking time, but such breakfasts also involve loads of prep work—making dough, batter, chutney, and needing loads of utensils, including grinders. Things can get really hard on working couples, especially women, with school-going children and parents at home.

How about rethinking and reconfiguring the entire ritual called breakfast? I gave myself this challenge one morning. My eyes fell on the papaya tree in our backyard, full of natural fibre, healthy nutrients and just enough sugar for basic calorie needs, but not so much as to trigger diabetes. Bonus, it was good for the stomach. When we got bored of papaya, bananas made an excellent alternative. Eggs are rich in protein and calcium. One whole egg is sufficient for an adult; I chose to discard the yolk and eat two egg whites instead, sometimes. Eggs and some fruits—trust me, that is enough, our body does not require more food for breakfast.

Why am I writing all this? The fact is that this is what we were eating for breakfast non-stop when we lived in Thiruvanathapuram. The papaya and banana trees in our yard were yielding fruits aplenty, and were the impetus for our new breakfast routine.

Our breakfast was healthy, with no added sugar or salt, and used zero oil. Mostly, there was no cooking required, just a bit of boiling at most (for oatmeal or eggs), and thus, less time was consumed.

I do loosen up during travel, and the point is not to be paranoid about eating. One cannot prevent ageing, but certainly one can make an effort towards ageing gracefully—this is what I believed in, and tried to influence my friends to take up exercise and healthy eating.

Just a few years back, I had moved to Thiruvananthapuram to take up a new job without knowing anyone in the city. Bini joined me later and we moved into a new neighbourhood without knowing the local language. But that did not make much of a difference. Six-plus years of time in an empty nest, and I can say with conviction that they were absolutely fulfilling.

My job warranted visits to the United States at least once a year. In addition, Bini and I continued to undertake personal vacations to the US to spend time with Shilu and Ashish, and meet quite a few friend families: Naba and Mamata, Kapil and Nidhi, Ravi and Deepa, Kuiyang and Feifei, to name a few.

We then completed a major personal milestone when Shilu got married to Kevin in Bhubaneswar, with reception dinners in my village as well as in Thiruvananthapuram. The wedding was nothing short of a fairytale. Kevin's parents, friends and relatives, as well as Shilu and Ashish's friends travelled all the way from the US. Shilu's best friend Kara and her mom Elizabeth, our friends Anjana and Anil, Nidhi and Kapil, Manasi and Sujit, Feifei and Kuiyang had travelled too. I slipped in a cultural immersion programme for them through a one-day trip to the Sun Temple in Konark.

Subsequently, Shilu completed her medical degree specializing in paediatrics, and joined a residency programme. In due course, she became a US citizen. Ashish also completed his undergrad programme in economics and joined a large finance corporation as a financial analyst. We, in the meantime, were deeply rooted back in India. Seeing both the children reasonably settled in the US, we decided to relinquish our green card.

I had also ticked quite a few items off our bucket list—family travel to Alaska and the Sundarbans, going with Bini to Andaman and Nicobar, Sri Lanka and the Maldives, and another family vacation—including Kevin—to Portugal and Spain.

'Are you planning to settle down in Thiruvananthapuram?' people used to ask.

'Looks like it,' we had begun saying.

And then, sure enough, God had different plans.

Just four months after relinquishing the green card, I was approached to move to the United States as the delivery centre head (DCH) of TCS's Global Delivery Center in Cincinnati, Ohio. We had to stand in the queue in front of the US Embassy to secure a visa again!

I was back in Cincinnati, the same city where I had first landed in the United States twenty-four years ago. By this time, it had become one of the cities most familiar to me, over multiple visits while working with GE Aviation. This time, I landed alone, at the onset of the winter, took a rental home, and was looking forward

to another long stint in the United States. How long? It depended
on how the job turned out to be, and how meaningfully I would
be able to engage with the new ecosystem. Bini joined me a month
later. Though I was not quite keen on moving to the US, the new
assignment, at least, was a welcome change, as the novelty in
my previous assignment had waned, and every new assignment
appeared with a bouquet of new learning imperatives. On the
personal front, at least we were closer to both our children, our
son-in-law Kevin, his parents Maureen and Thomas and of course,
many of our friends from our previous stints.

The job started on an enthusiastic note. 'Developing a robust
local delivery model for North America' was the ambitious
organization-wide undertaking entrusted to me. It called for
humongous data collation and analysis. My traits of enabling
people to collaborate without having supervisory control over
them came to the fore. The data collection and analyses were nearly
completed, and I was on target to draw meaningful inferences,
leading to large-scale implementation.

Quite unexpectedly, the global business climate turned sour.
The world came to a grinding halt due to COVID-19. Many of the
inferences drawn through the study could not be implemented
as the global business environment and workforce planning were
in flux.

International travel was shut down; even domestic travel
became a subdued affair. Workforce mobility was close to zero.
The entire industry was in a reactive mode. Companies asked their
employees to work from home, customers had no other option
but to agree—they were all in the same boat with the partnering
companies, grappling with the coronavirus.

Personally, I was never a big believer in working from home.
Not for any complicated reason, though—while in the midst of

serious thought about something from work, suddenly a question would hit me, 'shall I make toor dal or moong dal for lunch?'

After making a choice, you would think the matter would be settled. But no, a few minutes later, another question would arise, 'what would you prefer on the side, aloo chutney or baingan bharta?'

Not that my opinion would get serious consideration, but I could not escape without offering an answer.

But with COVID-19, there was no more conundrum about whether WFH was effective; it became the new normal. Companies had to adapt, work and workplaces were reimagined to facilitate employees to work from home. As the DCH, I had the imperative to ensure that the deliverables to the customers remained uninterrupted while paying heed to the health and safety of the employees.

A change induced in any ecosystem, especially on a macro scale, is both a challenge as well as an opportunity. Challenge, because change is hard initially, and is invariably associated with short-term dip in productivity. Opportunity, because it calls for agility, and spurs alternate thinking. There was considerable time-saving from commuting, which could be used to give shape to the ideas and dreams that had been put on the shelf, gathering dust.

I saw the silver lining, and began writing this book.

The TCS campus in Cincinnati, popularly known as the Seven Hills Park, is in the middle of 230 acres of forest. It has a few walking trails and a beautiful pond. The employees, over the past two years, had cultivated a summer garden. They had partnered with two local non-profit organizations that were providing food to the poor in the neighbouring communities. The produce from the summer garden was donated to those two non-profit organizations. I was curious to learn more about the garden where the season typically kicked off, with the first sapling on the annual Earth Day event in April, a ritual that had been followed during the two previous years.

With the virus mutating rather rapidly, no one was even sure about what preventive measures were truly effective. Soon, the paranoia about touch and sanitizing gave way to clarity about masks and social distancing. One opinion was consistent across different sections of people—the virus was lethal on those with poor respiratory systems. Well-ventilated outdoors were believed to be conducive for physical exercise, thereby improving the functioning of the lungs as well as blood oxygen levels.

This triggered something in my mind. I made it a regular practice to visit the campus, alone, on Tuesdays and Thursdays, and with Bini on the weekends. Trekking the trails and spending a couple of hours working in the garden were fun. My presence also motivated more employees and their families to join as volunteers. The three-thousand-square-foot garden footprint was expanded to six thousand. The most popular produce were tomatoes, cucumbers, peppers, zucchini, and melons. Eggplants, radish and beans complemented the spread. At my behest, a few desi vegetables: okra (bhindi) and bottle gourd (lauki) were added as well. We donated more than four hundred kilograms of vegetables and melons to the non-profit organizations that year. Close to a hundred pumpkins were harvested. The memory of employees and their families flocking to the garden for the final harvest, picking up pumpkins, and discussing Halloween pumpkin carving ideas has been etched in my mind. The commitment and indefatigable effort put in by a few of my colleagues—Konstantinos Elefter, Thomas Osborn and Priya Dayal, to name a few—was commendable.

COVID-19 had revealed one unadorned truth about humanity, that even the closest of friends were quite wary when it came to helping someone infected by the virus. Fear gripped the entire world, and travel was unreasonably restrictive. Fortuitously, we had developed a social ecosystem in quite short a time. We were fortunate to find our best friends in our immediate neighbours, a Marathi couple Shishir and Sakshi, and another couple from our Albany-New York days, Anil and Anjana, who by that time had moved to Cincinnati. Two of my colleagues, Shainu and Navneet and their spouses were also quite close to us.

I always believed that friends could be many, but real friends are few, and COVID-19 made every human being realize who was a real friend, and who was 'also' a friend.

The workplace ecosystem during the whole of 2020 was challenging, but it did not mean that one stopped trying. I took the plunge to influence the skillset mix of the employees in the Global Delivery Center. I noticed that the certification campaign, leading to the coveted recognition as TCS Contextual Master, had not gathered steam in the GDC. This is something that could be best accomplished while working from home—with this campaign, I started an initiative to build a pool of TCS Contextual Masters. The initiative paid rich dividends, both in terms of certification and recognition of experienced employees, as well as customers' perception about the GDC. One of my staff members, Navneet Matharu, played a significant role in driving this initiative.

Amid the uncertain business climate, we could sense the potential for growth. Boldly, we announced our plans[4] to expand our operations in Ohio by hiring more than 800 local employees at the Seven Hills Park campus and other offices across the state by 2022, to meet the evolving needs of customers. Adding 800 jobs may not sound big in the context of TCS, which employed more than 500,000 people at the time globally, but it was huge for the local communities in Cincinnati.

There was one more opportunity in the GDC where I thought of moving the needle—influencing the workforce pyramid. By spring 2021, COVID vaccines were available in the United States, and by summer, the rush for them had also decreased. I took the decision to support the summer internship initiative, in-premises training, and integration of freshers into a few customer engagements. The addition of a significant number of freshers at the bottom of the workforce pyramid significantly altered it for the better. The operations team, led by Konstantinos Elefter; the leader of the Internet of Things (IoT) lab, Brian Purvis; and the leader of the human resources team, Hannah Shobitha, played a stupendous role in this journey.

After receiving the second dose of the COVID-19 vaccine, we were back to our old habits. No more online shopping. One day, while in an Indian grocery store, we bumped into an Odia couple, Suvendra and Rasmita. They passed on word about us in the local community, and we got invited to the Raja Festival. As an Odia who has been out of Odisha for over three decades, the Raja Festival felt nostalgic. Shilu visited us that summer, and all three of us joined the celebrations. Shilu sang a Raja Festival song and won many hearts at the event. I also sang many songs. I was happy to see one more Odia, Arabinda Swain, who was an even bigger vocal music enthusiast than me. I noticed one thing: the Odia community in Cincinnati was small, but felt intimate. Over time, we became close to quite a few Odia families. A couple by the name of Anjan and Arpita had two beautiful and talented daughters, Isha and Lisa. Over time, both became our daughters-next-door. We will forever cherish our camaraderie with an elderly couple, Sukant bhaina and Itishree Nani, and a younger couple, Sandeep and Sowmya.

For a couple of years, the socioeconomic environment was strongly dictated by COVID-19. The Delta variant proved to be deadly and claimed many lives. The next variant, Omicron, though less lethal, turned out to be the most widespread around the world. Add to it the Russia-Ukraine war, and the world in 2022 was witnessing one of the most uncertain business climates in history.

Our visa was coming to an end, and I had no interest in reapplying for permanent residency or pursuing a visa extension. We had relinquished our green card three years ago because we never wanted to settle down in the US. It was not an impulsive decision; we had weighed our options. We had and continue to have stronger financial, social, and emotional ties with India. Moving away from Shilu, Kevin, and Ashish caused us heartache, but one cannot have everything in life. We wanted to associate ourselves with the larger ecosystem.

We have done the hard work and can afford visits to the United States whenever we want. Shilu and Ashish have deep attachments to their roots; knowing them, they will continue to visit us and our extended family in India. Even Kevin has been enjoying his visits to India so far. He has liked sitting on the floor cross-legged, has been refusing to use cutlery, and is eating with his fingers. He has enjoyed observing fishing at our farmhouse pond using fishing nets, and he has been getting used to eating fish with cartilage. There are no air conditioners at our village home, and he has not complained yet.

Some people find solace in sailing on two boats, but I personally find it too uncomfortable. We, therefore, sold our home in Cincinnati and headed back to Thiruvananthapuram, from where we had boarded our flight to the US three years ago.

12

THROUGH THE REAR-VIEW MIRROR

REMEMBER, ON MY VERY FIRST day of high school, when I was the laughing stock for wearing a red shirt—the only one I owned? Had a fortune teller gazed at my palm and predicted that one day, I would be an aeronautical engineer from IIT; climb through the ranks to become the first senior executive engineering leader for General Electric outside the US; a few years later, lead the talent development function of Tata Consultancy Services as its chief learning officer; that I would own three independent homes concurrently in Bengaluru, Thiruvananthapuram and Cincinnati; that I would own and drive BMWs and Audis; that I would be able to finance the college education of my children in the US without loans, I would have shaken my head in disbelief and said, 'Please tell me another joke, something that I can at least remotely believe.'

But all of this happened to me in due course. That is my life story, so far—many small stories wrapped in a large one.

A few more have faded from memory with time. Life is a journey, and we are in a state of permanent beta. Life and health permitting, I will continue to evolve in my profession for a few more years, and will strive to live a meaningful life until my last breath. More stories will unfold in the future.

There are many people who, like me, born to poor families, have made their way through life. My salute to them. At the same time, there are many others who could not make it. I want to tell them that it is never too late. If this book snaps some of them into action, I will feel that my effort in writing it has been worth everything.

Through the stories, I wanted to reiterate one point—that in the journey of life, I never let myself stay isolated. All along, I embedded myself into the ecosystem around me, drew energy from it, and used it as impetus to propel myself forward. I responded to the challenges that the ecosystem threw at me with resilience, without falling victim to it. I did it time and again; that is where some people falter. They see themselves as separate from the ecosystem, find faults in it, thereby accruing negative energy. That negative energy acts as slow poison; it holds people back from genuinely trying. By God's grace, and my parents' strong influence, I did not fall victim to this malady.

Not sure how or when, maybe the inspirational stories from mythology that my mother narrated to me worked on my mind subconsciously; I experienced self-awakening early on. Thereafter, I was driven by only one force: my inner conscience. I tried to influence and enable the ecosystem around me with laser focus and untiring actions, but whenever there was a moral conflict, I preferred to change myself by moving away to a different ecosystem; I never thought of tolerating a deterring ecosystem. Changing self is the hardest thing, and so, people try to change their circumstances, in vain. I did not subscribe to that philosophy; I preferred to change myself.

I was born to great parents. I was the beneficiary of Kaka's selfless love. For me, Rajuna was a godsent. Nuabou turned out to be a true 'new mother'. I did my bit to do well and got into government colleges with scholarships, but my siblings made their share of sacrifices to fund my education. There were inspiring professors who recognized the potential in me; I had the patronage of many great business leaders and bosses, who spotted me, lured, sometimes even pushed me into challenging and rewarding assignments. I latched on to those opportunities and repaid their trust with dedication and hard work, no doubt, but I would lie if I did not acknowledge the fact that luck did play a part. I was the right person at the right time, at least a few times.

While utilizing those opportunities to make it big, having a supportive family went a long way. In Bini, I found a life partner who sacrificed her career and took over my other responsibilities in entirety so that I could focus on my career. I could grab the opportunities whenever and wherever they came up and travel around within and outside India without worries because my parents were well looked-after by both my brothers at our village home—the biggest benefit of preserving a joint family. I have to give more credit to the ecosystem that enabled my growth, rather than say that I charted my path in life solely on my own. With all humility, that's why I wanted to tell my story, because that's the difference.

It is not that I did not face obstacles or come across disheartening and zealous people; sometimes even bosses. But I did a good job of closing my eyes to unsupportive and indifferent people. That's how I endured and overcame those obstacles. Banka bhai's lesson on what to remember and what to forget was timely.

Do I still remember and feel vindictive about any of the seniors who had tortured me during the ragging in engineering college? Hell no, time has healed those painful memories and blurred their nasty faces, but I still remember the face of that compassionate senior who picked me up on his bicycle and dropped me off at the hostel that morning in Rourkela. Alas! If only I knew his name! I would have met him and presented a copy of this book. I continue to admire and follow Sanjay bhai. I am still in touch with Basu, Suvash bhai, Amulya, Siba, Satya, Chitta and Ashutosh, among many other friends. I have resolutely developed the habit of remembering those who have had a positive influence on me, and forgiving and forgetting those who didn't.

It is also not that I never found myself at the receiving end of missed opportunities. It's not that I didn't face difficult situations; they needed to be managed with agility, without letting them affect my self-esteem and morale. 'When one door closes, another opens; but we often look so long and so regretfully upon the closed door that we do not see the one that has opened for us,' is a quote attributed to Alexander Graham Bell, and I believe in it. My innate nature of letting go of setbacks and looking forward to new opportunities with optimism continues to be my biggest strength. Habits like morning walks, jogging, singing, playing the tabla, gardening, travelling with family, talking to close friends, making new ones, and sometimes, just plain laughing things off—all help me recharge and bounce back.

Bou, under duress, had once reminded me there was no money plant growing at home. I was ignorant at that time, and did not know there was indeed an indoor creeper called money plant. Most houses have them. I also grow them in my home today. But a money plant does not grow money, one's karma does! The legendary Bill Gates has said, 'If you are born poor, it is probably not your fault. But if you die poor, it is certainly your fault.' Of course, Bill Gates has made enough money to say this, and people will listen to him. I certainly do not qualify to deliver such a quote, but one thing I would say about myself: barring the first few years of my professional career, I never felt that I needed significantly more money than what I had. It wasn't that, suddenly, there was an uncontrolled flow of money coming my way, but that I always had control over my needs and desires.

As a student in high school, a nine-inch-wide bench was enough to fall into deep sleep. In college, the hostel room's cot came as a privilege. As a newlywed, the narrower the cot, the better it felt. The problem for most people generally begins after this stage, as they fall into an old malady. Gradually a wider cot becomes a necessity, then two separate beds, then two separate rooms, and then maybe, two separate buildings. This is what wealth does to some people. I did not follow this trend. After joining my first job, it took me four years to buy a scooter, and fifteen years to own a house. Till then, we used public transport and lived in rented homes, but never chose to attain these personal milestones by taking loans. For someone born in more affluent circumstances, it is probably not a matter of debate, but for a scrapper, this debate is never-ending—whether to own and enjoy an asset acquired via loans, or observe restraint and build up enough savings to acquire the asset. I preferred to live a prepaid life, not a postpaid one. Borrowing never made sense to me. Whatever material possessions I could buy with my own savings gave me and my family true happiness, as at any point in my life, I had only assets, not liabilities. This helped me develop a mindset of richness amidst scarcity.

It is futile to try to describe Rajuna's influence on my career and life in words. He continues to inspire with his philanthropic endeavours, and I derive immense pleasure in contributing whatever little I can to support him financially. One of my actions will continue to give me bliss for the rest of my life—I hosted him in the US, so that he could visit his places of interest. As a staunch devotee of Swami Vivekananda, he was keen to visit the

Art Institute of Chicago, where Swamiji delivered his famous 'Sisters and Brothers of America' speech. Rajuna was also keen to visit Vivekananda Cottage, at Thousand Island Park in New York. Accompanying him, I was fortunate to visit both these places of great historical importance, which I probably would not have without him. I also reminisce about my family and me accompanying him and Mani Bhauja to Swami Vivekananda Rock in Kanyakumari, the Meenakshi Temple in Madurai, and an overnight houseboat experience in Alleppey.

Nuabou continues to be like my new mother. To fulfil her vow, I bought her a necklace at the earliest possible opportunity. Bhaina remains the head of our joint family. Though I lived far away from my village for the most part of my career, my siblings as well as Bini's and their respective families remained part of our lives—they have strong family bonds to Bini, me and our two children.

I feel blessed that I was able to take Bou and Nana on a pilgrimage to the Char Dham, beginning with Rameswaram. At the end of the trip, Bou reminisced about the time I had pleaded with her to take me to see the Ram Setu that the monkeys had built, the place where Lord Rama had blessed the squirrel. I have no memory of having made such a plea, but apparently, I was very little and kept bugging her. So, Bou had consoled me by saying that it was an impossible dream: there were too many rivers to cross, dense forests to trek through and high mountains to climb. We could never reach it!

She finished reminiscing by saying, 'In my wildest dreams, I could never have imagined that the same son would grow up one day to take me not only to Rameswaram, but also to the other three dhams.' By the time she finished, she was wiping tears from her eyes. What else could be more gratifying to a son like me?

Bou had intervened at the right time by telling me not to solicit any favours from anybody, unless it was absolutely unavoidable. She had also expected me to repay the loans I had taken without her knowledge, before taking admission to engineering. I never forgot that, nor did I want it to make it look like a simple loan repayment. I felt indebted, so I did it my own way.

Rohit Mamu's son was struggling for a job after completing his engineering degree; I hosted him and coached him until he got a nice job. When we lived in Chennai, we hosted Bhikari Mamu and Mayin (aunt) at our home, accompanied them to the Tirumala Tirupati Devasthanam, and at the time of their departure, gave them a lump sum amount to help their elder son start a business. I was waiting for the right opportunity to pay the debt received from Pisa (Rajuna's father), and when Rajuna wanted to construct a classroom at the school in the name of Pisa, I funded its construction.

A debt, however small it is, is a debt after all; I get better sleep after paying it.

Then, there are many unsung heroes; Mala, our housemaid in Bangalore; driver Babu; the caretaker of the Thiruvananthapuram guest house, Sambhu, to name a few. I will always be there alongside them in their good and bad times; they were among the top of the list of invitees to Shilu's wedding.

My personal accomplishment, in my view, is not my rags-to-riches story; it lies rather in the story of my evolution—entering an unknown ecosystem, receiving from it, merging into it, and gradually growing within it to reach a level of comfort and security, so as to start influencing it. That is why I continue to derive satisfaction, especially, from two stints in my career. One, beginning a start-up joint venture and growing it non-stop over a period of close to a decade to employ a large number of youth of India, also impacting the elementary education of hundreds of poor children in the neighbourhood through the EISA project; and two, using the role of the chief learning officer of TCS to impact the quality of employment—through skill and competency building—of hundreds of thousands of young talents. The feeling of giving back and adding value to society or an ecosystem cannot be described in words.

It would be difficult to make a detailed plan for my future, as God always has a Plan B. However, I have a guiding principle: whatever I do for the rest of my life will have something to do with school education, primary healthcare, environment, professional skill development and enabling employment potential of unemployed youth in our society.

One expedition humans don't really tend to go on is on an exploration of the self. It starts with self-awareness and self-belief; the rest is about giving it a try. That is how I learnt to make and fly kites, sing, run a full marathon, raise a beautiful family, make some money, and impart some positive influence on the ecosystem around me. Time will tell how the rest of the journey will pan out. As I said, in an enlightened moment, 'Life is after all a journey, not a goal. It is a continuous function till a point of discontinuity precipitously appears someday somewhere. And whenever that point of discontinuity appears, I hope I will have a moment to pause, smile, wish good luck to my fellow passengers, and whisper to myself—what a ride it was!'

ACKNOWLEDGEMENTS

THIS BOOK WOULD NOT HAVE seen the light of the day without the help and inspiration from many people. The list is rather long, but I feel indebted to mention a few. My sincere thanks to: R. Gopalakrishnan for introducing me to HarperCollins India.

One of my idols, S. Ramadorai, for accepting my request and writing the foreword of this book.

My colleagues in Tata Consultancy Services, who inspired me to write. P.R. Krishnan (PRK) and R. Gopinathan for calling out my writings at times, causing embarrassment and instilling confidence at the same time.

Many of my colleagues at General Electric, especially of John F. Welch Technology Center, Bangalore, for having partaken in my leadership journey.

My ex-colleagues, Dolon Gupta and Nidhi Singh, wholeheartedly, for editing the manuscript of this book at different stages.

Smitha Balakrishnan, Sanu Khan and my daughter Suhasini (Shilu) for editing some of the anecdotes in this book.

To Praveena Pramod, for patiently organizing the URLs of the blog posts that I published in different points in time. Many of those posts served to some extent, as the building blocks of this book.

My son Suman (Ashish) for creating the spark in me by making me read the personal statement for his college applications.

My wife Sairindhree (Bini) for keeping me on my toes by asking 'when will the book work be over?'

To Emmanuel David and Prof. Gopal Pr. Mahapatra, for being among the few friends with whom, without any strings attached or hesitation, I keep bouncing off my thoughts and solicit inputs, including the very idea of writing this book itself.

Sachin Sharma, associate publisher at HarperCollins, for his patience. He changed the course of this book two times. Each time I thought I was done, he made me start all over again with the stroke of just one (constructive) comment!

Shreya Lall, senior editor at HarperCollins, for copyediting and proofreading the book.

Last, but not least, the readers of this book: the proceeds from your patronage will go towards laying the foundation stone of a charity, in memory of my loving parents.

REFERENCES

Scan this QR code to access the detailed references

INDEX

Aarif, 145, 151

Abate, Vic, 151

accelerated learning, 137

aerospace engineering, 115–116, 120, 132, 210

Agadhu Sir, 47–48

agricultural land, 3, 5, 9, 32, 103

Ajit, 149

Akshaya Sir, 31, 41, 59

Allen, Woody, 170

Anbarasu, 153–154

Anjan and Arpita, 208

applied mechanics, 96–97

Apuja bus stop, 73, 88

articulation, 190, 196

Art of Articulation, 190

ASCENT, leadership programme, 184

Ashish (son), 163, 166, 174, 195, 202, 209; alphabet reversals, 160; fear of losing, 161; as financial analyst, 203; MathCounts and Science Bowl competitions, 173; stray dogs, 162; at University of California, 198

Ashok, Praveen, 185

Ashutosh, 213

Asia Pacific American Forum (APAF), 171–172

Asim, 149

aspiring, 52, 149, 176

Association of Talent Development (ATD), 193

Aswathi, 179

attestation, 64

attrition, 151

Atul, 149
automation, 135, 200
Awaar, Krishna Murthy, 190
Aziz, Aarif, 151

Babu, 216
Balakrishnan, Smitha, 183
Bangalore (now Bengaluru),
    120, 122, 124–125, 127,
    129–134, 137–139, 143, 149,
    156, 161, 171–172; as India's
    Silicon Valley, 170; Odisha
    Cultural Association, 166
Bangalore Engineering Centre
    (BEC), 150, 182
Banka Bhai/Banka Sahu, sweet
    shop owner, 127–128, 133,
    212
Banshidhar Sir, 30–31
Baskaran, B., 140–141, 149
batchmates, 29–30, 46–47, 49,
    52, 55, 86, 93–94, 96, 100,
    103, 116–117, 121, 124;
    Amulya Prasad Panda,
    98–99, 141, 213; Ashutosh
    Dash, 97; Chittaranjan Patra,
    97–98; Manoranjan, 101; Om
    Prakash Prasad, 118; Satya
    Narayan Panda, 98, 112, 213;
    Siba Charan Pradhan, 97
Behera Babu, 125–126, 130
Bell, Alexander Graham, 213
bell-bottom pants, 81, 99

Bhaina and Shyama, 133
Bharathi, Usha, 183
Bhikari Mamu and Mayin
    (aunt), 216
Bhubaneswar, 105, 113, 131,
    197, 202
Bijayaram Mausa, 97–98
Bijay Mamu, 44
Bilasuni, 27, 32–33, 79, 81;
    Shri Gopaljew High School,
    28–29, 31, 36, 42, 66
Bini (Sairindhree Mohapatra-
    wife), 27, 29–30, 109–113,
    126–127, 129–139, 159, 163,
    168, 171–172, 174, 176, 198,
    202–204, 215; consenting
    marriage, 108; father as
    secretary of school, 42;
    meeting at college, 105–106;
    painting, 199; pursuing MA
    in Sanskrit, 105; smile of, 84;
    as teacher, 130; visiting in
    her hostel, 84, 109
Biswal Bhaina, 130
BITS Pilani, 88
blog posts, 181–182, 188, 191,
    196
boarding charges, 38, 41
Board Pokhari, 37, 70
Bombay (now Mumbai), 135
books, 34, 36, 77 (see also
    writing); textbooks, 70, 78,
    164; company of, 82

borrowing/loans, 9, 38, 76, 103, 210, 214, 216; short-term, 76, 103

breakfast, 49, 71–72, 100, 126, 152, 168, 201–202

B.Tech., 115

Burra, R.V., 96

business relationship manager (BRM), 137

Capture Their Hearts award, 156

Caudill, Corbett, 140, 144

Chandra, Maya, 148

Chandrasekaran, N., 140, 144–145, 176, 185

Charan Sir, 45

Char Dham, 163–164, 215

chemistry class, 69–70

Chief Human Resources Officer (CHRO), 156

Chief Learning Officer (CLO), xiii, 182, 192–193, 210, 217

Chitta, 213

chivda (flattened rice) from, 72, 75, 77, 81, 152

Choudhury, Bipin Bihari, 86

Cincinnati, 203, 207–210; TCS campus in, 205

civil engineering, 93, 109, 114–118, 121

'co-creating capabilities,' 187

college: applications, xiv, 63; hostel, 78, 106, 172; see

also engineering colleges; Ravenshaw College; Regional Engineering College (REC), Rourkela

community development, 154

computational mechanics, 124

computer-aided design (CAD), 134

conversion projects, 134–135

COVID-19, 204–208

creativity, 24, 78, 148

crops: crops, 9, 102; rabi, 102, *see also* paddy

Cuttack, 2, 5, 44, 49, 64, 68, 71, 73, 79, 84, 88, 93, 101–102

CXO, 185

Daley, Sharon, 156

Dama, xv, 29–30, 39–41, 48, 55, 58, 61, 85, 104

Das Babu, 130

Das, Rabinarayan, 86

Das, Sanjay (Sangeet Samrat), 95–96

Dayal, Priya, 206

Dayalan, Sarulatha, 190

debate, 56–57, 80, 214

Deepthi, 154, 193

delivery centre head (DCH), of TCS's Global Delivery Center, 203, 205

Dharani Bhai, 53

dhenki (device to separate rice grains, 13–14
digital learning platform, 187
discipline, 36–37, 58, 79, 169; of children, 168
dreams, 52, 78, 99, 115, 117, 119, 133, 139, 198, 205, 215
Dutta, Manasi, 174
Dutta, Nivedita, 162

EACoEtsav, 143, 147
ecosystem, 124, 175, 180, 205, 209, 211–212, 216–217
Ehteshami, Mohammad, 151
Ek Duuje Ke Liye, 94
Electric Group Company Limited, China—Shanghai, 171
electricity, xv, 4, 70
Elefter, Konstantinos, 206, 208
Elfun Initiative for School in Agrahara (EISA), 155, 217
empathy, 16, 23, 74, 153
employee advocacy, 145, 151
empty nest syndrome, 198
'enabling certainty,' 187
engineering colleges, 87–89, 91, 138, 212
Engineering Analysis Center of Excellence Pvt Ltd (EACoE), later as Bangalore Engineering Centre (BEC), 139–145, 149–150, 182

Engineering Recognition Day (ERD), 144, 146–147
English, 52–53, 55, 72, 84; daily newspaper, 118; essay type questions, 54; medium of teaching, 79; spoken, 94–95
entertainment, 4, 83
environmental engineering, 107, 109
ERD theme, 146–148
exams, 23–25, 27, 34–35, 43, 45, 51–53, 55, 57–61, 77–79, 86–87, 96–97, 99–100, 112–113, 115–116, 168–170; board, 55, 58, 169; engineering entrance, 90; English, 60; GATE, 113, 115; high school board, 23, 35, 45, 90, 112; Intermediate, 86, 88; internal, 78–79, 81, 96; Navodaya, 156; Rural Talent Scholarship, 27; semester, 99–100; state JEE, 87

family: Ashish (son), 136; Babu, 97, 116; Bhaina, 5, 7–9, 15, 17–18, 23–25, 33, 36–38, 51–52, 59–60, 66, 68, 72–73, 75–76, 86–88, 92, 100–104, 111; Bhikari Mamu (Bou's younger brother), 92; Bijayaram Mohapatra (Mausa), 91; Bijoy Mamu,

35; Bou/Maa, 4–11, 13–17, 23–24, 32, 34, 36–38, 59, 68, 74–76, 85–87, 90–93, 111–112, 129–130, 132–133, 163–164, 215–216; feuds, 9; Gita, 97, 116; Goli Mausi, ('maternal aunt'), 91; Kaka, 4–5, 7–9, 15–17, 22–26, 32–33, 37, 51, 59, 68, 80–81, 148; Khudi (aunt, Kaka's wife), 32, 37, 59, 68; Mani Bhauja, 37, 40, 52, 58, 60, 81, 215; maternal grandfather, 17; Mitu (youngest sister), 32, 68, 75–76; Nana/father, xiv–xvi, 4–5, 7–9, 11–13, 16–18, 22–25, 28, 30, 32, 38–40, 43–44, 59–61, 73, 75–76, 85–87, 111, 132–133, 162–163, 182; Nuabou (sister-in-law), 37–38, 59–60, 68, 70, 72–76, 85, 87, 90, 92–93, 100–105, 108, 111–112, 114, 122, 132; Pisi Nani, 28; Raja (baby nephew), 122, 130; Rita (younger sister), 7–8, 12, 15–16, 68, 75–76, 85, 112, 129–130; Rohit Mamu (Bou's adoptive brother), 5–6, 216; Rosy (baby), 112; Samir, 91, 97, 116; Sanjunani, 5, 7–8, 12–14, 16–17, 24, 32, 34, 36–37, 60, 148; Shyama (younger brother), 22, 68, 75–76, 85, 136, 197; travel, 203

farm, betel leaf, 8–9, 13, 16, 22–24, 32–33, 35, 39, 52, 81, 102, see also crops

fatherhood, 158–159

festival, 4, 9, 16, 108, 167, 198; Dahi Handi, 118, 191–192; Diwali, 118; Dussehra, 6; Ganesh Puja, 20–21, 45, 166; Janmashtami, 118; kite-flying during Raja, 17; Onam, 198; Raja, 17, 52, 60, 103, 208; Rakshya Bandhan, 97; Saraswati Puja, 4, 83

'first time' experiences, 70, 84; away from children, 198–199; bus travel, 5; as class topper, 45, 109; in college, 70; eye contact with Bini, 109; footwear, 59; photograph, 63; pillion ride, 125; a room for self, 104; train travel, 101

5A framework, 187

fishing, 15–16, 24, 32, 198

flood, 9, 86, 101–103

footwear, 16, 59, 66; chappals, 59, 65, 93

friends: Acharya, 125–126, 130; Ajai, 172; Akbar, 172; Anil, 172, 207; Anjana, 172, 207; in Bangalore, 125; Bhikari,

61, 84; Bidyadhar, 34, 61;
Deepa, 172, 202; Feifei, 172,
202; Garima, 172; Hemant,
25–27; Kamesh, 172; Kapil,
172, 202; Kuiyang, 172, 202;
Manoj, 33, 42, 61; Mansi,
172; Nafis, 172; Nidhi, 172,
202; Nihar Babu, 125–126,
130; Praveen (Patnaik), 125;
Ravi, 172, 202; Soujanya,
172; Sudhir, 46–48; Sujit, 172
frugal leadership, 137
fund raising from relatives, 92,
see also borrowings/loans

Gali, Pravin, 152
Gandhi, Indira, assassination
of, 114
Ganesh, Sharada, 183
Ganguly, Sourav, 161
Gates, Bill, 213
GDC, 207–208
General Electric (GE), 137,
140–142, 144–146, 154,
156–157, 170–171, 174–175,
210; aviation, 150; Aviation
Leaders Day event, 156;
Energy Headquarters in
Schenectady, 170; Global
Engineering, 151
Gilchrist, Adam, 161
Global Delivery Center, 207

global leadership meeting
(GLM), 156
Global Learning Calendar, 184,
193
Goddess Jagulei, 1–2, 4
Goel, Ravi, 140, 144
Golap, 109–110
Gopal Bhai (Bini's elder
brother), 31
Gopinathan, Rajesh, 190
Grameshwara Mahadeva, 2–4,
59; temple, 1, 62
grandparents, xvi, 163
Grant, R.H., 140
gratitude, 62, 65, 77, 127, 166
growth agenda, 146
Gunupudi, Laxmi, 142
Gupta, Dolon, 190
Gurukul, 185; virtual, 186

habits, 7, 11–12, 43, 57–58, 80,
82, 85, 100, 107–108, 197,
200, 208, 213
Hampi, Virupaksha Temple, 167
Handa, Archana, 151
Hangzhou Steam Turbine
Company Limited, China,
171
Harbin Electric Company
Limited, China, 171
hard work, 34, 42–43, 53, 55, 67,
79, 135, 138, 147, 209, 212

Hari, C.K., 145

Hemachandani, principal, 160, 181

high school, 28, 30–34, 36, 40, 42, 45, 62, 66, 68, 72, 81, 173, 175

Hindustan Aeronautics Limited (HAL), 120, 122, 125, 133–134, 138

Hindustani Classical music, 162

Hiranmay, 149

hobbies and habits, 200–201

hospitalization, 195

hostel, 36, 41, 68, 70–72, 75–76, 84–85, 87–88, 93–94, 96, 99–100, 102, 105, 109–111; mess, 41, 71, 75, 103; own room in, 104

humongous data collation and analysis, 204

ICU, 178–179, 181

IIT, 115–119, 121, 123, 210; Kharagpur, 116–118, 120; prospectus, 115

IIT-JEE, 86–88

ILP curriculum, 192

India Engineering Centre, 151, 170

initial learning program (ILP), 142, 192

inter-caste marriage, 108

Internet of Things (IoT), 208

iQlass network, 186–187, 192

irrigation engineering, 109, 112

Isha and Lisa, 208

Ispat General Hospital (IGH), 98

Jagatsinghpur, SVM College, 66–67

Janardhan, S., 192

Jaswinder, 149

Jena, Kshitish Ranjan, 112, 138

Jha, Rajkishore, 185

job: interview, 121; placement scenario, 115; situation, 114

John F. Welch Leadership Development Center in Crotonville, 156

John F. Welch Technology Centre (JFWTC), 144–145, 150–152, 156–157, 174–175, 182

Joseph, Saji, 192

journey, 51–52, 58, 61, 112, 158–159, 180, 185, 190, 194, 197, 208, 210–211, 217

Jyotsna, 84

Jyotshna Madam, 55, 57

Kailash, 46, 56

Kaka, 25

Kaliaghai Hata, 32, 61, 73
Kantapada, 19, 31; school, 19–20
Kanth, Vikram, 151
Karthik, Dharshana, 185
Karthik S, 190
Kasarda High School, 59–60
Kesavasamy, K., 200
Kevin, 202–204, 209
Kharagpur, 93, 116
Kites flying, 17–18, 60, 85, 115, 119, 217
Krenicki, John, 171
Krishna, 141
Kuruvilla, Nivedita, 193

Larsen & Toubro, 175
Lava Kusha, musical drma, 26
Leadership Development Institute (LDI), Trivandrum, 193
LEAPVAULT CLO summit, Tata Institute of Social Sciences, 193
learning and development (L&D) at TCS), 182; global head of, 176
learning management system (LMS), 185
learnings, 11–12, 17–18, 54, 137, 139–140, 170, 178, 181–189, 191–193, 196, 219

Leena, 151
Light Combat Aircraft (LCA, later as HAL Tejas), 122, 130
LinkedIn, xiii–xiv, 181
love, 10, 13, 34, 37, 85, 106, 130, 145, 196, 201, 222
love marriage, 108
Love Story, 94
'low hanging fruits,' 196
Lynch, John, 156

#MMT, 196
#MondayMorningTrivia, 196
Madan Bhai, 31
Madras (now Chennai), 136
Mahalingam Sir, 136–137
Mahanadi river, 71
Mahapatra, Prashant, 117
Mahapatra Babu, 130
Mala, 216
Mallick Bhaina, 130
Mallika, 141
Malur, Rajashekhar, 154
Mamata, 202
Maria, 149
marriage, 38, 100, 104–105, 110, 127; proposals, 110
mass communication, 150
mathematics, 41, 52–54, 56–57, 72, 79, 83–84, 89, 96; Set Theory in, 72, 84
Maureen, 204

Mausa, 88, 91, 93–94, 97–99, 103, 116

meal/eating/food, 23, 37, 72, 99, 102–103, 131, 180, 202; breakfast, 202; with fingers, 209; fish, 15–16, 23–24, 32; 'gina tarkari', 24; hostel mess, 75; 'kulthi bean', 102–103; Mani Bhauja serving, 37; Nana correcting, 11–12; pakhala, 15, 25, 74; tamarind pickle, 24; as working bachelors, 126

medical entrance exams/ medical JEE, 89, 91, 171

Menka, 151

mischiefs, 38, 46–49, 52

Mitsubishi Heavy Industries, 175

Mohanty, Happy, 141

Mohawk Hudson River half-marathon, 174

'money cannot buy happiness', 131

money plant, 74, 82, 213

mother, 5, 15, 19, 56, 211

motherhood, 159

motivation, xvi, 52, 127, 194

motorized vehicles, 19

M.Tech, 115–117

Mukherjee, Pranab, 193

Munjal, Sunil Kant, 193

mythology, 10, 56, 211

Naba, 202

Nabaghana Bhaina, 97

Naik, Suvash Chandra, 93

Nair, Col., 178

Nanda, Alok, 147, 149

Nanda Bhai, 124–125

National Cadet Corps camp, Chandikhol, 44

National Institute of Technology (NIT), 91

National Talent Search Examination (NTSE) Scholarship, 67–68

Navneet, 207

necklace, 103–104, 215

new clothes, 21, 30, 79, 84

Niagara Falls, Manhattan, 137

Niali, 49, 63–64

Nidharshana Narayanan, 185

Nisha, 141

novels, 35

NTSE scholarship, 73, 77, 83, 86, 99, 103

A Nuhen Kahani, 65

numerical problem solving, 86, 96

Odia: medium school, 53; movie, 49, 65, 83

Odisha, 2, 4, 17, 67, 91, 93, 108, 208

Odisha Cultural Association, 130

Odisha state engineering JEE results, 89

Odisha State High School Certificate Board Examination, syllabus for, 52

Old habits die hard, 11

Omicron, 209

one-on-one discussions, 196–197

'Operational Excellence through Six Sigma and Digitization,' 146

organization, 142, 145–148, 154, 185–187, 192–193; as human pyramid, 191

Osborn, Thomas, 206

Oshi Maushi, bath soap from, 22

'PACT of small talk,' 154

paddy, 13–14, 25, 86, 102; cultivation, 22–23, 33; for higher education, 86, see also crops; farm

Padhi, Balakrishna (nana), 4

Padhi, Suman Kalyan (Ashish), xiii

Padhis, 4, 52

Paina Nana/ Paiana (Rajun's youngest brother), 37–41,

45–46, 54, 58–59, 62, 67–68, 71, 79, 83, 113

Panampilly, Suresh, 192, 200

Panda, Basudev (Basu), 72, 79, 83–84, 86–89, 97, 213

Panda, Mahavir, 117

Pandit Sir, 46, 55, 180

pantry, 153

Parida, B.K., 119, 138

passport size photographs, 63, see also 'first time' experiences

Patnaik, Pranab Kishore, 26, 65, 108, 143, 166; in Bangalore, 166

Patnaik, Praveen, 127, 130

Paul, Debtanu, 185

peer-learning, 191

people versus process conundrum, 140

Philips radio, 26, 32, 64,81

Pisa (Rajuna's father), 39–40

poems, 52–53, 56, 134

'practice makes perfect,' 58

Pradipta Sir, 54

Prasan, 141

Prasant, 199

Praveen, Patnaik, 126

Premila, Gino, 192

primary school, 7–8, 24, 26–27, 31, 33, 56, 59; curriculum, 25; schoolmates, 28, 32

privacy, 5, 104
privileged backgrounds, 82, 158
Priyanka, 156
product-technology-process
    ecosystem, 146–147, 151
projects, xvii, 134–135, 142, 184,
    192; in fracture mechanics,
    119, *see also* Light Combat
    Aircraft (LCA, as HAL Tejas)
public sector undertakings
    (PSUs), 120, 133
punishments, 37–38, 44, 46, 49,
    103, 154
Purohit, Veena, 185
Purohit Babu, 125–126, 130
Purvis, Brian, 208

ragging, 93–97, 212
Raghavendra, Anupama, 185
Rai, Menka, 151
rainy season, 2, 20, 31
Rajasekhar, 155
Rajuna/ Rajkishore Dash,
    headmaster, 28–30, 36–40,
    42–44, 47–54, 57–59, 61–62,
    66, 81–83, 108–109, 111, 124,
    127, 215–216; family, 36; gift
    from, 59; quarters, 38, 40–41,
    45, 60, 62, 81; wife, Mani
    Bhauja, 37
Ramadorai, 138, 140, 144–145,
    176

Ramakrishnan, Suraj, 183
Rashmi, 57
Rasmita, 208
Ravenshaw College, 61–63,
    65–67, 69, 82, 89, 92–93,
    97, 99, 152; campus of, 68;
    medium of instruction, 71;
    New Hostel, 67–68
red shirt, 29–30, 66, 210
Regional Engineering College
    (REC), Rourkela, 87, 90–91,
    93, 97, 109, 115, 141; annual
    inter-college spring festival,
    107
resources, xv–xvi, 23, 33, 158
Rice, John, 156
ritual, 2, 6, 15, 21, 24, 37, 88,
    108, 151, 201, 206; of writing
    to Bini, 113
rivers crossing, 66–67, *see also*
    floods
Rosario, Jeanne, 151
Rourkela, 90–91, 93, 97–98, 101,
    107, 112, 117, 121, 213
Roy, Bidisha Sinha, 190
Russia-Ukraine war, 209

Sahijwani, Leena, 151
Sahu Bhaina, 130
Saju, 179
Sakshi, 207
Sambhu, 216

Sandeep and Sowmya, 208

Sanjay Bhai, 96, 213

Sanju, 97

Sanskrit, 54–56, 60, 105, 180

Satpathy Bhaina, 130

scarcity, 5, 23–24, 46, 82, 214

Schenectady Central Park, annual park-cleaning event, 171

school uniform, 29–30, 32

self-awakening, 211, 217

self-belief, 85, 217

self-development, 77, 117

self-discipline, 82

Selvaraj, Swarnasudha, 185

Senior Executive Band in GE, 156–157

Seven Hills Park, 205, 207

Shainu, 207

Shedd, John A., 162

Shilu (daughter), xiv, xvii, 130–131, 133–135, 137–139, 160–166, 170–176, 195, 199, 208–209; and Ashish managing police man, 167–168; Gandharva Mahavidyalaya exams, 162; illness—urinary tract infection (UTI), 158–159; marriage with Kevin, 202; maths problem, 169; Medical College Admission Test (MCAT), 173; New York Medical College, 198; in paediatrics, 203; Union College, Schenectady, 173; wake-up call from, 172

Shishir, 207

Shobitha, Hannah, 208

Siba, 213

Singh, Jagjit, 143, 166

singing, 26, 30–31, 44–45, 52, 70, 83–84, 95, 143, 162, 166, 213; bathroom, 100; Odia bhajan, 26, 30

sketch, 78

social currency, 99

software companies, 120

Software Development Capability Maturity Model, 141

Soniya, 156

Sreedhar, M.K., 130

Srinivasa Rao, B.S. (BSSR), 123, 130, 138

Stanley, Rick, 151, 156

State Board Exam results, 61

steam turbine engineering, as general manager of, 170–171, 175

Subair P.H., 183

subjects: aerodynamics, 118, 121; aerostructures, 121; Computational Aerodynamics, 119; propulsion, 118

Suja, 97
Sukant Bhaina and Itishree
    Nani, 208
summer garden, 205–206
Sundar, 149
Sundaram, Maria, 147
Sushama Nani, 97, 116
Suvash Bhai, 93, 97, 104, 213
Suvendra, 208
Swain, Arabinda, 208
Syiji, 179

talent: development, 187–189,
    191–194, 210; ecosystem,
    187–188
'talking the walk,' 190
Tata Consultancy Services
    (TCS), xiv, 134–143, 180,
    182, 185–187, 190, 194, 200,
    210, 217, 219: Bhubaneswar,
    197; colleagues, 141, 191;
    Contextual Masters, 207;
    and GE, 140, 144; guest
    house, 139; ILP, 183, 192;
    intellectual property,
    192; KNOME, 181, 188,
    191; L&D strategy, 184;
    Thiruvananthapuram, 176,
    193, 198; Xplore, 192
team, 118, 125, 135–136, 140,
    145–146, 148–150, 161,
    182–184, 188–190, 192, 194

Thakur, Rohit, 151
Thiruvananthapuram, 142,
    177, 183, 198–199, 202–203,
    209–210
Thomas, 204
three As concept—Awareness,
    Articulation and
    Amplification, 190
toilets, 71, 75, 78–79, 113, 129,
    132, 155
training, 148, 184, 192,208
trains, 93, 101, 131–132, 191;
    travel without ticket (WT),
    101
Trinatha mela, 4, 26, 52, 60
trunk, as companion, 36, 38, 60,
    68–70, 88, 116, 122, 171
trust, 34, 45, 85, 138, 145, 183,
    202, 212
tuitions, offering, 103
Tulo, Ajit, 175

Ultra Mega Power Project
    (UMPP), Tata Power, 175
Uma Maheswari, 149
United States, 137, 170,
    173, 175, 203, 208–209;
    permanent resident card
    (green card), 173; visits to,
    136, 202

University College of
    Engineering (UCE) Burla,
    91–92
Upendra sir, upper primary
    school headmaster, 27
Uttarakhand, 164

vacations, 85, 131, 202
Vaira, 149
Vijayaraghavan, G. of KIMS
    Hospital, 178
village (Mahanga), xv–xvi, 1–4,
    8, 13, 15, 19–20, 35, 38–39,
    52, 59–60, 62–63, 85–86,
    101–102, 113, 131, 133–134,
    197–198; 'danda,' 2–3; game
    of marbles, 3; Hensanaga
    pond, 3, 15–16, 25, 70, 75,

129; Marichia Nali, 3, 19–20,
    31, 74; rainy season, 2
Viswanath, Sadanand, 161
volunteering, 38, 155–156, 206

wake-up calls, 160, 172, 180–
    181
'walk the talk,' 190
wedding, 127; at Bini's home,
    129; Chauthi Rati, 129
WFH, 205
Whitefield, 139, 154, 170
Wille, Guillermo, 151
working bachelors, 126
working from home, 204, 207
writing, 195–196
wristwatch, 72–73, 77

ABOUT THE AUTHOR

Damodar Padhi has more than thirty-five years of experience in aerospace, energy and IT consulting. A graduate of the department of aerospace engineering at the Indian Institute of Technology, Kharagpur, his passions include creating and nurturing high-performing, business-enabling teams and developing a pipeline of leaders.

During his tenure as the chief operating officer of the GE Infrastructure engineering division in John F. Welch Technology Centre, Bangalore, he was recognized with the Capture Their Hearts award at the 2004 GE Aviation annual leaders' day confluence in Cincinnati, Ohio, for excellence in people leadership.

As the chief learning officer of Tata Consultancy Services, he conceptualized and championed 5A learning and inclusive-learning pyramid concepts within TCS, and evangelized them in global talent-development forums. Known for proclivity in social learning, he was recognized as the TISS-LEAPVAULT global CLO of the year 2014, as the CLO of the year, in 2017, by the international CLO magazine and the Stevie Awards best employer CLO of the year 2018.

HarperCollins *Publishers* India

At HarperCollins India, we believe in telling the best stories and finding the widest readership for our books in every format possible. We started publishing in 1992; a great deal has changed since then, but what has remained constant is the passion with which our authors write their books, the love with which readers receive them, and the sheer joy and excitement that we as publishers feel in being a part of the publishing process.

Over the years, we've had the pleasure of publishing some of the finest writing from the subcontinent and around the world, including several award-winning titles and some of the biggest bestsellers in India's publishing history. But nothing has meant more to us than the fact that millions of people have read the books we published, and that somewhere, a book of ours might have made a difference.

As we look to the future, we go back to that one word— a word which has been a driving force for us all these years.

Read.

Harper
Collins

HARPER
PERENNIAL

HARPER
BUSINESS

HARPER
BLACK

हार्पर
हिन्दी

HarperCollins
Children's Books

HARPER
DESIGN

HARPER
VANTAGE

Harper
Sport